12/89

W9-BFQ-222

KLEE

Klee

BY DENYS CHEVALIER

CROWN PUBLISHERS, INC. - NEW YORK

Title page: THE ARTIST AT THE WINDOW (Der Zeichner am Fenster), 1909
Watercolor and chalk, 12″ × 9⅗″ (17.6 × 16.3 cm)
Collection: Felix Klee, Bern

Collection published under the direction of:
MADELEINE LEDIVELEC-GLOECKNER

Translated from the French by:
EILEEN B. HENNESSEY

Library of Congress Cataloging in Publication Data

Chevalier, Denys.
  Klee.

  (Crown art library)
    1. Klee, Paul, 1879-1940 — Criticism and interpretation.
  2. Painting, German.   3. Painting, Modern — 20th century —
  Germany.   I. Title.   II. Series.
  ND588.K5C45   1988   759.9494   88-444
  ISBN 0-517-50302-6

PRINTED IN ITALY – INDUSTRIE GRAFICHE CATTANEO S.P.A., BERGAMO
© 1979 BONFINI PRESS CORPORATION, NAEFELS, SWITZERLAND
REVISED EDITION

RESORT (Kurort), 1913. Watercolor, 3¾″ × 7″ (9.5 × 17.8 cm). Saidenberg Gallery, New York

The birth of Paul Klee near Bern in 1879 came soon after the rise of the Impressionist movement in France, where Van Gogh, Gauguin, and Seurat were about then making their first appearances. Klee's father Hans, a German national and a teacher at the cantonal Teachers' Training School, and his mother, a woman of French and Swiss origins, were both musicians. They already had a daughter, Mathilde, three years Paul's senior.

In elementary school and later in high school, the future artist proved to be talented but, for lack of diligence, a mediocre student: languages, literature, poetry, music, and drawing were the only subjects that interested him. He hesitated over the choice of his future career. Should he become a poet? (He had more or less secretly committed to paper several short stories and poems.) A musician? (In truth, everything seemed to predestine him for this career, for he was already playing the violin with the Bern Symphony Orchestra.) An illustrator? (He was not yet thinking of painting.) His strikingly liberal parents did not influence him in any direction; when the time came, he himself would have to decide.

The time came in 1898, just after he had received his high-school diploma. At this point, for the first time, he refers to himself as a "future painter." However, young Paul was aware

HAMMAMET WITH MOSQUE (Hammamet mit der Moschee), 1914
Watercolor, 8″ × 7½″ (20.5 × 19 cm).   Collection Heinz Berggruen, Paris

RED AND WHITE CUPOLAS (Rote und weiße Kuppeln), 1914
Watercolor, 5¾″ × 5⅜″ (14.6 × 13.7 cm).   Kunstsammlung Nordrhein-Westfalen, Düsseldorf

of all that he lacked: precision of observation, correctness of draftsmanship, experience — in short, the foundations. In his wisdom and modesty he did not even think about expressiveness or personalization of style. But the horizons of Bern, it seemed to him, were too circumscribed to satisfy his nineteen-year-old's eagerness. Where should he go to acquire the knowledge he lacked? Paris? He thought about this for a short time, but Paris was far away, and although he knew French, he was not at ease in it. And the reputation of Paris as the "modern Babylon" (as exaggerated as it was widespread in the German-speaking countries) was not likely to arouse the enthusiasm of his family.

Having weighed the matter carefully, he settled on Munich. It was perhaps smaller and more provincial than Paris, but it was only half the distance from Bern; he would feel less out of his element there, and at that time it was, if not a cosmopolitan artistic metropolis, at least an important cultural center that would offer him good music as well as instruction in art. In the capital of Bavaria, where he arrived in October 1898, he witnessed the triumph of Art Nouveau: Certain of his drawings, influenced by the magazine "Simplicissimus" — "the most beautiful magazine in the world," he claimed, undoubtedly for lack of elements of comparison with what was being done elsewhere — tended to resemble that new style. At this period he became acquainted with Endel, Eckmann, and Obrist, all thoroughly second-rate artists of local interest, but he still knew nothing of Monet, Pissarro, Van Gogh, Cézanne, or Gauguin.

After preparing at Knirr's private art school for his entrance into the Academy of Fine Arts, he entered Stuck's class at the Academy. It was a disappointment to him; he did not learn to paint, as he had naïvely hoped, but for days on end toiled through dreary sessions with a model. The works he produced during the three years he spent studying in Munich were merely academic exercises faithful to the principles taught him. However, certain landscapes and occasional humorous drawings (one landscape of the Elfenau is reminiscent of Corot) done during his vacations surpass the level of the merely conscientious and skillful, thanks to the introduction of several simplifications.

Klee experienced extreme difficulty in transposing his expression from the poetic to the plastic, and in integrating the third dimension into the plane. During his early years his excursions into the domain of color were rare; he devoted himself above all to drawing, and inaugurated that very distinctive style, at once philosophical and satirical, which was to characterize his work until around 1913. To this style belong those subsequent fantasies, more often cruel than comical, in which the human body, in accordance with the saying of Novalis that "humanity is a comic character," is treated with a kind of mockery.

Discouraged by Stuck, Klee made an unsuccessful attempt to join the class of the sculptor Rümann. He had better luck with Ziegler, who taught him the rudiments of etching. This technique seemed to him a wonderful medium of expression because the operations it required, although numerous, permitted the artist to modify the appearance of the engraving each time. In Klee's opinion the engraving was therefore superior to the drawing, whose lines were direct and final, in several important ways: a line in an engraving could always be improved or changed,

Woman in a Deck Chair (Frau im Liegestuhl), 1911
India ink, 6″ × 9¹⁵⁄₁₆″ (15.2 × 25.2 cm).   Paul Klee Foundation, Museum of Fine Arts, Bern

and there were innumerable openings for the unexpected and for the exploitation of the fortuitous.

We have now come to the first milestone in the life of the painter, an event which was to act less as a revelation on his art than as an initiation and a promotion in his training.   This was his discovery of Italy.   Between the end of October 1901, and the beginning of May 1902, he visited Genoa, Leghorn, Pisa, Rome, Naples, Florence, and other cities, in turn enchanted by the Florentine Gothic and repelled by the Baroque.   He passed by Piero della Francesca, Giotto, Simone Martini and Paolo Uccello, but admired Raphael, Leonardo, Botticelli and, somewhat less conventionally, early Christian art.   In particular, he realized that architecture is a genuine medium of plastic expression, and that careful study of it could help him to progress in his own research, for what he was seeking was, in the last analysis, the revelation of the very foundations of art.   In Rome he also saw for the first time an exhibition of sculptures by Rodin. He was not familiar with modern art (moreover it was not what he had come to

Italy to look for), and despite the powerful impression it made on him he was later to confess that "modern art disconcerted me to such a point" that he found Rodin's modeling "caricatural."

Back home in Bern, his style became more distinctive, undoubtedly under the influence of the sketches brought back from his trip of drawings and tempera and fresco paintings. However, it is not yet possible to speak of a "personal style of expression." From then on he was to work alone, except for his attendance at Strasser's class. Despite his absorption in art, Klee did not abandon any of his intellectual activities of the preceding years; paralleling his readings in the masterpieces of world literature, he continued to practice the violin, and frequently traveled with the municipal orchestra of Bern, of which he was a member. Obviously these two stimuli, which were for him much more than hobbies, did not fail to exert a certain influence on his plastic activity.

Painting inspired genuine timidity in him. He ventured into it only step by step — his son Felix later remarked that "color only slowly and prudently penetrated the formal element" — and for the time being he abandoned it deliberately, in a sense reserving it for a future date. The always lucid artist recognized that "color appears in my work only as an embellishment of the plastic impression." The knowledge of his shortcomings, however, engendered not renunciation but, on the contrary, an increased determination, which by developing extremely precise plans for gradual moves and achievements that would link up with and strengthen each other, was to enable him to reach his objective with a kind of unerring logic. His efforts were thus directed first and foremost to drawing and etching. In his bitterly comic satirical drawing, he attempted to reconcile subject and object, combining realistic vision wih a subjective interpretation. In his etching (in which, again, he superimposed psychic intentions on natural structures) he studied in particular the various methods and techniques: bites, grainings, textures, and so on — in short, "the tricks of the trade." In any event, the year 1902 saw the beginning of the series of fifteen etchings (chiefly zinc-plates, with a few copperplates) that constitute the major portion of his graphic work. This series, which was completed in 1905 — one etching dates from 1901 — is by virtue of its homogeneity generally regarded as of greater significance than the forty plates that the artist was to create between then and 1932. Klee destroyed a great deal of the work he did before 1903, and with the exception of these etchings, his early works — academic pieces, landscapes somewhat in the style of Corot, and illustrations in the flowery style of Art Nouveau — should be regarded above all as preparatory exercises. The universally famous etchings known as the *Inventions* (*The Virgin in the Tree*; *Two Men Meet, Each Supposing the Other to Be of Higher Rank*, etc.), the fruit of constant modifications, of successive versions, and of innumerable retouches in order to obtain an increasingly intense line, came into being at this time. Certain aspects of his style (not the best ones) offer analogies with those of Beardsley and William Blake, but possess a keener sense of the grotesque and a very characteristic humor. Moreover, his disordered imagination, restrained by a demanding, meticulous, even finical reasoning, reminds one of that "Angel of the Bizarre" common to both Baudelaire and Poe. For Klee, however, plastic representations must never start from a preliminary poetic speculation but from the establishment of figures whose calligraphy is capable of symbolizing his ideas.

Around 1904, after a visit to the Print Room in Munich, he felt particularly close to Goya (the *Disasters of War*) and then, in 1905 and to a lesser extent, to Félicien Rops. Earlier he had admired a group of paintings by Corot at the Rath Museum in Geneva. His forms, real and imaginary, meticulously put together and elaborated, have an unusal epigrammatic quality. Satire — a satire which Klee made very explicit, not only in the titles he gave his works but also in his written descriptions of them — always pierces through the allegory. Was he afraid that the plastic language alone would prove incapable of representing the totality of their content? He nevertheless notes that "Drawing and writing are basically identical" — a statement strangely reminiscent of the slogan of an artist's correspondence course, "If you know how to write, you know how to draw."

Klee's conception of beauty is derived not from the object but from the sensation aroused by its deformation or, more precisely, by the re-forming invention. He respects the basic features of the anatomy he had so conscientiously learned. The morphological evocation does not spring from poetry; it is the opposite which occurs, vicariously. The vision controlling his expression being metamorphic in nature, the vegetal, animal, mineral, and human are fused therein. Thus limbs become branches, bud, and fingers, and vice versa. Klee passes from the allusion to the symbol by trusting to the virtues of instinct. It is as if his pencil or his etching needle were themselves freely inventing the roads they trace over the surface, like Leonardo, whose spirit of invention fed on the cracks in a wall. Klee would never cease to cultivate (if not domesticate) these unconscious forces of expression to their outermost limits. He himself said that he was "stripped of my day-to-day self" and "all calm at night." He did in fact frequently work at night, in a small room in a middle-class apartment. While "the moon, itself similar to a dream of the sun, reigns over the world of dreams," the still nocturnal atmosphere so propitious to the concentration of the intellectual faculties abolished for him the frontiers between dream and reality. While his plates still show traces of Art Nouveau, they are already related, by their resonance, to the spirit of the German Romantics: Achim von Arnim, Novalis, Jean Paul, Eichendorff, Brentano, and Schlegel. It was not an accident, then, that six years later he was to entitle one of his works "Scene from a Hoffmann-like Tale."

In his line, in which the norms of classical beauty are constantly challenged, pessimism and desolation are united with a startling innocence. Klee was quick to combine these qualities with color and a new technique that he had developed himself: glass painting. This innovation, the result of numerous experiments and much trial and error — he began by coating a pane of glass with tar and then scraping white lines on it — was to make possible a rejuvenation of the "classical" style of his engravings. Scratching plates, experimenting sometimes with watercolor and sometimes with oil painting, constantly extending the range of his methods, he simultaneously liberated his style and envisaged the direct translation of nature. To be sure, it is not yet possible to discover from his work that, as he was to record in his diary, "the meaning of the word impressionism, which had been foreign to me until then, was brought closer to me by the efforts made to achieve a total expression." But the school of nature — he "toils over the motif" — put him on the road to color, light, and space.

For approximately a year the painter was to work assiduously at the discipline of glass painting, and its materials were to enrich his vocabulary considerably. The glass paintings, although still more or less satirical in spirit, are very different from the etchings. In conception they resemble the drawings and watercolors done in the same period. Among the observations that can be made about them is the fact that the play of values clearly dominates the study of the colors. The painter was to express himself sometimes in a vein taken over from the caricatural and grating style of the earlier years, with a touch of mannerism, sometimes in another, almost populist style, finally arriving at that *Little Garden-Picture* of 1905 whose chromatic, compositional, quite "Matissean" figures have been pointed out in every analysis of the work. (Klee, however, was not then acquainted with Matisse, and only later was to call him "all things considered, the painter of today.")

If perchance he had an inkling in this period of his life of the works of the Expressionist group of "Die Brücke" (Bleyl, Kirchner, Schmidt-Rottluff, and others), who were surfacing in Dresden, he probably did not know that in Paris the Fauves (Derain, Marquet, Matisse, Vlaminck) had succeeded the Postimpressionists and the Symbolists and the Nabis, who were the offspring of Gauguin. For in Bern Klee lived in almost total seclusion, except for frequent meetings

Voltaire, Candide, chapter 15: "place, place pour le révérend père colonel!", 1911
India ink, 4¾" × 9¹⁄₁₆" (12 × 23 cm). Paul Klee Foundation, Museum of Fine Arts, Bern

1919. 193.

NEW FORTRESS (Festungsneubau), 1919
Watercolor, 6¾″ × 5⅞″ (17.2 × 15 cm).   Private collection, New York

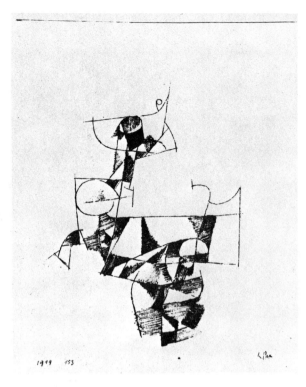

Without Title (Ohne Titel), 1914
India ink, 7″ × 5⅜″ (17.8 × 13.6 cm)
Paul Klee Foundation, Museum of Fine Arts, Bern

with an unchanging band of comrades. Whatever the human or artistic warmth in other areas of the family environment, it was in solitude that he forged both his language and his destiny, with infinite perseverance in his determination and in his insight into the study of esthetic problems.

In Paris, which he visited for the first time in the spring of 1905, he frequented above all the Louvre and the concert halls. He admired Watteau, Chardin, Leonardo (whom he was rediscovering), and Goya (who enchanted him), but took no notice of any modern artist, and his private notebooks remain silent on this subject. Undoubtedly he did not have the time to go to see them. (He would have to go to Basel in order to admire, during a later trip, the works of Monet, Degas, Carrière, Manet, and Renoir.) However, whether it was the result of his trip or the simple consequence of his normal intellectual development, he notes that he has understood that "it is not by drawing on the forms of an idea, not originally plastic, that one arrives at pure art. I doubt that this possibility exists for me."

The autumn of 1905 saw the beginning of a new creative state. Klee believed, with Goethe, that genesis is more significant and important than creation, and that becoming is superior to being. He therefore tried to isolate the poetry in the vital flow of artistic development, that is, to discover the "germ of life giving birth to itself" (Novalis), or what the Latin writers had already referred to as "natura naturans." In his etchings of this period, form and ideas tend to flow together. They are less allegorical than formerly and are denuded of all worldly superficiality *à la* Beardsley. They do not demonstrate, they exist.

In 1906 Klee adopted the aquatint method and, after a short trip to Berlin, finally achieved his first success: ten of his *Inventions* were exhibited at the Munich "Sezession." This compensated to a certain extent for his lack of success in his attempts at collaboration on various periodicals — failures which were to be repeated constantly over the period of a decade, for Klee was not easily discouraged. Yet he had all the requisite qualities of an excellent newspaper illustrator — a biting, sharp line, expressiveness of distortion — and his work is reminiscent of Munch and Lautrec. Only the blindness of newspaper publishers can account for the fact that all of them declined his offers of service.

14

IMPRESSION OF TEGERNSEE (Eindruck vom Tegernsee), 1919
Watercolor, 11½″ × 7⅝″ (29.9 × 19.4 cm).   Private collection, New York

SHRUB IN THE THICKET (Kleiner Baum im Gebüsch), 1919
Oil, 12⅝″ × 9¹⁄₁₆″ (32 × 23 cm).   Collection Lady Nika Hulton, London

Among the books that made a deep impression on him at this time, there was one which, transcending the level of cerebral appraisal, was to accelerate the development of his style. This was "Candide," which immediately aroused his enthusiasm. ("I have read a totally unique book: Voltaire's "Candide.") This work was to hold him spellbound for years before he decided to illustrate it. True, for the time being, he was preoccupied with other matters. In September 1906, at the age of twenty-seven, he was married in Bern to a young Munich girl named Lily Stumpf, and the newlyweds then departed to settle in Munich. Thenceforth, and for a period of about fifteen years, it was Lily who had the responsibility of keeping the family (which was enlarged the following year by a son, named Felix) alive, thanks to the music lessons she gave at home and in the city. The family settled in a modest three-room apartment in Schwabing, the Montmartre of Munich. Here Klee had only a minimum of space — a mere corner — in which to do his drawing, etching, and painting. This undoubtedly explains why he confined himself of necessity to small pictures, and also why we find in his language a tendency toward miniaturization and a kind of fluctuation, as if an esthetic conception, like a lode or deposit, after having been systematically mined was slowly exhausted. At this time the slenderness, elegance, and preciosity of his line sometimes border on the decorative. However, lack of space could not permanently hinder him or seriously hamper his pursuit of a fundamental unity between himself and the world. Over the years the kitchen in which he worked was to become a kind of laboratory in which the most complex techniques — rubbings, colored inks, mixed media, etc. — one by one came into existence. Moreover, Klee was in possession of his own interior space, and no living conditions, no matter how wretched, could alienate him from it.

Relatively quickly, thanks to an increasingly close and constant confrontation with nature, he was to liberate himself from the crisis that threatened to affect his art, and to liberate his spaces from the formalism that was threatening them. As a corollary, his line came to life, perhaps under the influence of Daumier and still more that of Ensor, of whom he had heard from one of his friends. Just as optical reality reintroduced a breath of fresh air, "pure art tends toward Impressionism," he noted at this time.

In short, except for the matter of color — for his glass paintings and watercolors, with their generous washes, are often black and white — he was quite close to the Impressionist credo; he told the Swiss draftsman Welti, who invited him to participate in an exhibition of the Federation of Illustrators (where, strangely enough, he was refused admission), that, "I thought I belonged more to the Impressionists, at least to judge by my current works." He was already trying to integrate the notion of time (moment and duration) into his spatial expressions, an attempt that he was to pursue for a number of years. His move to Munich promptly bore fruit. He visited two Van Gogh exhibitions, which familiarized him with the work of that painter, and he read with profit Van Gogh's correspondence. In certain of its aspects Van Gogh's work confirmed him in his opinion that calligraphy is the most important component of the picture. (Basically, he was a draftsman more than a painter, though he was soon to say that "my calligraphic illustrative style is finished and done with." He was therefore grateful to the Dutch painter for showing him that there exists "a line which at once benefits from and surpasses Impressionism." In this connection it must be borne in mind that the 9,146 items which make up the total body of Klee's production include only 761 paintings on canvas, not all of which are oils. In any event, it is certain that his drawing *Head of Young Man with Pointed Beard (Self-portrait)* seems to be directly under the influence of the Master of Auvers. Van Gogh frightened him a little. Klee's temperate, orderly nature and his temperamental inclination toward careful planning obviously could not come to terms with an art so violently and continually paroxysmal. "I see clearly that it is genial, but the pathological side is quite disturbing."

On occasion Klee quite appropriately made use of binoculars, as much to liberate himself from the naturalistic perspective as to capture his models from life. Consequently it is not surprising that he viewed Cézanne as "the master *par excellence*." His constructive line corroborates and in a sense lays the foundations for his own conception of the composition, and his color creates volume. Several of Klee's works — *Self-portrait, Full-face, Head Resting in his Hand*, and *The Artist at the Window*, (see title page), also a self-portrait — testify to his lively interest in the activity of the father of the Cubists, who had passed away three years earlier.

In this period the artist's visual experiments indicate how anxious he was not to founder in imitative representation, "the chief disadvantage of naturalistic painting, to which I constantly return in order to complete my apprenticeship and research." He attempted to eliminate the local colors from his palette while considering the pure color area as a privileged element of chromatic harmony. Paradoxically, however — but Klee is no stranger to contradiction — he perfected a quasi-automatic chiaroscuro method that consisted of gradually adding black, in a series of layers, to already painted surfaces. But in other ways, and despite several quantitative determinations in the graduation of the chiaroscuro by the establishment of tonal values, he is nevertheless close during this period to Cézanne and Matisse, with a kind of foreboding of the discoveries of Seurat and Delaunay, neither of whom he had ever seen. His *Girl with Jugs* reflects the painter from Aix-en-Provence, "who is likely to inspire me much more than Van Gogh," with colored areas reminiscent of Matisse and the 1905 *Garden Scene* that we have already mentioned. However, it would not be advisable to exaggerate the importance or the significance of these few examples, which are too open to interpretation. Now and henceforth, whatever the claims made by his modest nature, the essence of Klee's production was to be found on an authentically personal level, and the outside influences, sifted, assimilated, and transposed, must be regarded as negligible.

The artist was now thirty-one years old. In his representational graphic works, line is subdivided into formal contours and, perhaps, by enlargements of elements observed with the magnifying glass, into autonomous signs. In order to study infinitely small objects, morphologies in formation, and embryonic mechanisms, he made his vision penetrate the interior of objects. In his "Fragments", Novalis remarks that "the idea of a microcosm is the highest for man (we are all cosmometers). It is highly probable that a singular mystique of numbers also appears in nature, as it exists in history. Is not everything wondrously significative and symmetrical, all concatenations and illusions?" In Klee's works the images of nature in gestation tend to gradually replace those of nature fulfilled. By the fall of 1911 he had become one of a group that included some of his former schoolmates in Bern side by side with a few new faces: August

Needle Drawing (Nadelzeichnung), 1919
6″ × 9½″ (15.2 × 24.1 cm). Private collection, New York

Macke, Franz Marc, Vassily Kandinsky, Marianne von Werefkin, Alexis Jawlensky, Gabriele Münter, and a few others, including Hans Arp, who even more than Klee belonged to two cultures.

A short time earlier he had begun to prepare a complete and profusely detailed catalog, a kind of daily inventory, of everything he had produced and was producing, down to the smallest sketch. He was also working on the illustrations for "Candide," a project that was to continue for another year.

His admiration for Goya gave way to a burst of enthusiasm for El Greco — an El Greco who was somewhat caricatural, famished looking, and as if in decline. His drawings no longer evoke people but silhouettes, half-insect, half-greyhound, frail, filiform and disembodied, refined of all bulk and encumbering flesh.   Because of their elongated limbs and tiny, insignificant heads, one could take them for praying mantises or grasshoppers.   Here line becomes the interpreter of a psychology.   Thus Klee succeeds in translating not so much the text as the spirit of Voltaire, in accordance with his very discerning judgment on the writer's style: "In "Candide" there is a higher element which fascinates me: the precise expression, with this precious economy, which characterizes the language of Voltaire."   It is undoubtedly this same faculty of intimate, transcendent understanding that later, toward the end of his life, justified his smooth accession to the beauties of the world of Racine, a world that is inaccessible to non-Frenchmen.   He once again came to grips, in his investigations into tonality and luminosity on the one hand, into calligraphy and structure on the other, with the problems of nature.   Being a poet, philosopher, and naturalist, as well as a painter, he went beyond his experiments in black and white and polychromy and studied (but on a level different from that of the Impressionists) the effects of the light that nibbles at contours, bends lines, deforms perspectives, and eats away colors.

Houses Near Oberwiesenfeld Parade Ground Outside Munich
(Häuser am Exerzierplatz Oberwiesenfeld bei München) 1910.   India ink, 7⅞" × 18¾" (20.1 × 40.7 cm)
Paul Klee Foundation, Museum of Fine Arts, Bern

PICTURE OF A TOWN WITH RED AND GREEN ACCENTS (Städtebild), 1921
Oil, 17⁵⁄₁₆″ × 17⅛″ (44 × 43.5 cm).   Private collection, Switzerland

VILLA R, 1919.   Oil, 10¼″ × 8⅝″ (26 × 22 cm).   Museum of Fine Arts, Basel

Full Moon (Vollmond), 1919.   Oil, 19¼″ × 14½″ (49 × 37 cm).   Otto Stangl Gallery, Munich

BATTLE SCENE FROM THE COMIC-FANTASTIC OPERA "THE SEAFARER"
(Kampfszene aus der komisch-phantastischen Oper "Der Seefahrer"), 1923
Watercolor and oil, 14¾" × 20⅟₁₆" (37.5 × 51 cm)
Private collection, Switzerland

24

On his second visit to Paris, two years before the war, he visited the galleries of modern art — Barbazanges, Durand-Ruel, Bernheim, and Kahnweiler — looked at the work of Constantin Guys and, more attentively, at the canvases of Braque and Picasso, and then visited the studios of Le Fauconnier and Delaunay. The latter made such a strong impression on him that he not only painted, some twenty months later, an *Abstraction — Colored Circles with Colored Bands*, which is clearly inspired by the inventor of Orphism, but in addition had a (quite mediocre) text by Delaunay, "on light," published in the periodical *Der Sturm*, in Klee's own translation.

Upon his return to Munich, Klee exhibited in the second "Blue Rider" exhibition with Kandinsky, Alfred Kubin, Franz Marc, and Gabriele Münter. The series of illustrations for "Candide" was being finished. His drawing was now becoming diversified, simultaneously acquiring schematizations that were almost oneiric in nature and inventions that resembled childish scrawls. The world of childhood does in fact belong to that primeval world that the artist, once he had glimpsed and then reached it, would never cease to exploit so magnificently. "I would gladly give up action, passion, composition and everything else if you could open up to me with roseate keys the country of the child's mysterious thoughts," says Ludwig Tieck, a statement echoed by Novalis with greater conciseness: "Where the child is, there is the Golden Age."

The definition of the origins of expression certainly obsessed him, and he dreamed of reaching that absolute point zero from which he could make his real start, reconstruct creation, and launch his message. In his painting he was making greater use than before of contrasts, combining them chromatically within quantitative and qualitative hierarchies. Paralleling this, the arrangement and distribution of colored areas sanctions in the work the ideas of plastic space and time within which the movement is accomplished. It seems clear that it is the passage from one state to another, a process not only of metamorphosis but also of transition, that opposes him to the Cubists, a large portion of whose program he nevertheless approved of. In his quality as an apparently consistent romantic he was to write in 1914: "Ingres, they say, is supposed to have organized repose. I should like, beyond pathos, to organize motion." But less than two years later, by a kind of return swing of the pendulum that scanned his spiritual life, and among innumerable other contradictions of the kind that are resolved only in the very opportune cosmic swooning of the soul, he claimed in one and the same breath that "pure motion seems to me banal. The temporal element must be eliminated," and regretted that he could not express the "faint mists before the star penetrates. The moment, difficult to paint, is so fleeting."

The fact remains that at this time (1912) the equilibrium he was seeking in his art was at once absolute and fluctuating ("I begin rather by melting into the All"), for the world of his investigations is that of the intermediate states, limbos of a sort in which permanence can be perceived only dialectically and oppositionally, through a shifting atmosphere in which creatures belong completely neither to the world of the living nor to that of the dead. In 1913, in a desire to restore the atmospheric evanescence, he painted various watercolors: *In the Quarry, Rain Threatening a Small Landscape,* and others. As in several later works (*Shifting*

Landscape, 1920; *Before the Snow,* 1929) he examines nature in ferment, in transformation. His plastic motivations were now following much more closely in the path of the Impressionists than in that of the Cubists and Futurists, whose exhibitions he had seen in Munich a short time before.

After a winter of confinement to Bern on account of illness, in the spring of 1914 the painter unexpectedly had the opportunity to take a second journey, which was to prove as important as his earlier Italian trip for the acceleration of his creative capacity and the developments that would grow out of it. He went to Tunisia, and it was there that he discovered the East, which won him over from the very beginning. Here he was to be confronted with a new kind of light and a new palette. In the sketches he painted from nature, his palette became brighter, and he was soon to exclaim: "Color has taken hold of me." Sensation was, in a sense, the fixed pivot around which his expression gravitated. In the same period, however, his grasp of the virtues of construction increased in power; through these virtues and through their geometric rigor he moved away from the anecdotal picturesque. (See, for example, the quadrangles of the rooftops and façades of the small, cubic native dwellings in *Hammamet with Mosque* on page 6.) At last he found a use, this time in a contemporary language, for his memories of plastic organization, architectonic in nature, that he had brought back from Italy; moreover, this strikingly transcended the pictorial plane, for the observation of the numerical hierarchy that presides over architectural construction led him into more general reflections on the methods of growth and proliferation used by nature in her manifestations. At Carthage the artist reestablished the link between past and present, as he had already done when he stood before the Roman ruins. "What a destiny is that of the bridge between the here and the beyond, the bridge over the frontier of yesterday and today."

Klee was back in Munich by the time World War I broke out that summer. Having passed what was then the age of active duty, he was not for the time being called up. In the three small, dark rooms of his apartment he organized his ideas, sorted out his papers and notes, and worked intensively, in turn drawing and painting, often by artificial light. He was continually varying his materials and techniques, overlapping his color planes. He painted in oils on various fabrics seemingly the least suitable for this purpose — muslin, linen, and canvas — that he prepared himself with stucco or chalk. For his watercolors, distemper works, and drawings he used cardboard, wood, and paper of various textures, not always of good quality; these too he sometimes prepared himself. He scraped, washed, and brushed in order to increase his effects, traced drawings on backgrounds painted with watercolors, varnished the still-damp paper of certain pastels, and combined media and glued bases of contrasting textures one on top of the order. Needless to say, with the passage of time the result, at least in some cases, is that the inks have faded, lines have disappeared, and panels have come apart. This explains the infinite precautions taken by the Klee Foundation in Bern when it brings these very fragile and delicate works out of its files — which it does as seldom as possible.

It is certain, however, that the pursuit of these experiments contributed to a considerable broadening of Klee's pictorial methods. While his kinship with the Impressionists became tenuous — in 1915 he remarked that Impressionism was "one area of which I now retain only

Head Jugglers (Kopf Jongleure), 1916
Pen and ink, 6¾″ × 5½″ (17.2 × 14 cm).   Private collection, New York

memories" — his relationship to the Cubists was being clarified. His investigations into materials were a continuation of the paintings with sand and twine and the "papiers collés" of the painters of the Paris school. Moreover he used, after the fashion of the Cubists, an oval format for his *Hommage to Picasso* (1914), and his principles of surface organization were not without analogies with analytical Cubism.

At the end of the second year of the war, new, graphically determined forms appear on the overlappings of the generally light-colored planes in his watercolors. These are figurative elements which herald the later picture-poems, ideograms, and cosmic symbols, and through which the acquisitions of his Tunisian experience continue to be revealed. At this time he met Franz Marc, with whom he had until then been corresponding regularly, for the last time. He remarks of his colleague and friend, with deep regret, that "as an officer he had plenty of time to spend on his personal appearance, and he had even adopted the bearing of an officer. His new uniform was becoming to him — I shall even say 'unfortunately' very becoming. Was he or was he not still the old Marc? I am not sure..." Disappointed in his opinion and genuinely saddened, Klee remarked two or three months later that "Marc and I are no longer corresponding since his last furlough." In March 1916, Marc was killed in action. It seems indeed that the spiritual and intellectual development of the two men had followed very different paths. Klee himself had come a long way from the good chauvinist Pan-Germanist who had declared in 1902 that "today more than ever I believe in salvation by the Teutons, all the more so since Germany could not be assimilated into the Latin culture. And if we do not succeed in germanizing Russia, the immediate future will belong to her," and, a short time later: "Oh, what deeds are done by the soul — and by the German soul above all others!"

In his thirty-seventh year the artist received his draft notice. The King of Bavaria, a worthy descendant of Ludwig II and a patron of scholars and artists, saved him from the trenches, and he was assigned in turn to supply dumps, an airplane factory, and a treasury office, in Landshut, Schleissheim, and Gersthofen. His relative freedom permitted him at least to draw with reasonable regularity, if not to paint, although he did make use of certain types of airplane canvas covers for the latter purpose. In addition he occasionally sold one of his works. After reading some Chinese poems, he added touches of watercolor to symbolic forms, like ideograms and calligraphic works, which are as so many spiritual propositions. Then came his "picture-poems." The vocabulary of these metaphors consists of crosses, circles, arrows, and sometimes letters and numerals in the style of Braque, who had introduced them into painting. The expression of these works, which tend to be picture-puzzles, becomes esoteric. "Art does not render the visible, it makes visible," Klee was later to declare. By a kind of method of association, in which the form is determined by a preliminary idea of the world, they bear witness to the Cosmos. And, since the vision in which they originate transcends the immediacy of objects, they are linked to the original formative mechanisms, the genesis.

At Christmas of 1918 Klee came home on furlough, and in January 1919, he was discharged. Back in Munich, he worked in oils much more frequently than before, perhaps to give the lie to his reputation as a miniaturist, which was a source of some irritation to him. He painted very free compositions, like the *Shrub in the Thicket* (see page 16), landscapes in particular,

MAIN SCENE FROM THE BALLET "THE FALSE OATH"
(Hauptszene aus dem Ballet "Der falsche Schwur"), 1922
Watercolor, 19″ × 12¼″ (48.2 × 31.2 cm).   Private collection, New York

DREAM CITY (Traumstadt), 1921
Watercolor, 18⅞″ × 12³⁄₁₆″ (48 × 31 cm).   Private collection

1921/100. Der Opsüer vom hohen C

THE ORDER OF HICH C (Der Orden vom Hohen C), 1921
Watercolor, 12¾″ × 9¹⁄₁₆″ (32.5 × 23 cm).   Penrose Collection, London

LANDSCAPE WITH FULL MOON AND QUARTER MOON
(Landschaft mit Vollmond und Viertelmond), 1923
Watercolor, 4½″ × 11¾″ (11.5 × 29.9 cm)
Private collection, New York

32

LANDSCAPE WITH YELLOW BIRDS
(Landschaft mit gelben Vögeln), 1923
Watercolor, 13⅞″ × 17¼″ (35.5 × 44 cm)
Private collection

Tomcat (Kater), 1923
Watercolor, 9⅝″ × 14″ (24.5 × 35.5 cm)
Private collection

SERPENTINES (Schlangen Wege), 1934
Watercolor, 18¹¹⁄₁₆″ × 25″ 647.5 × 63.5 cm)
Private collection, Bern

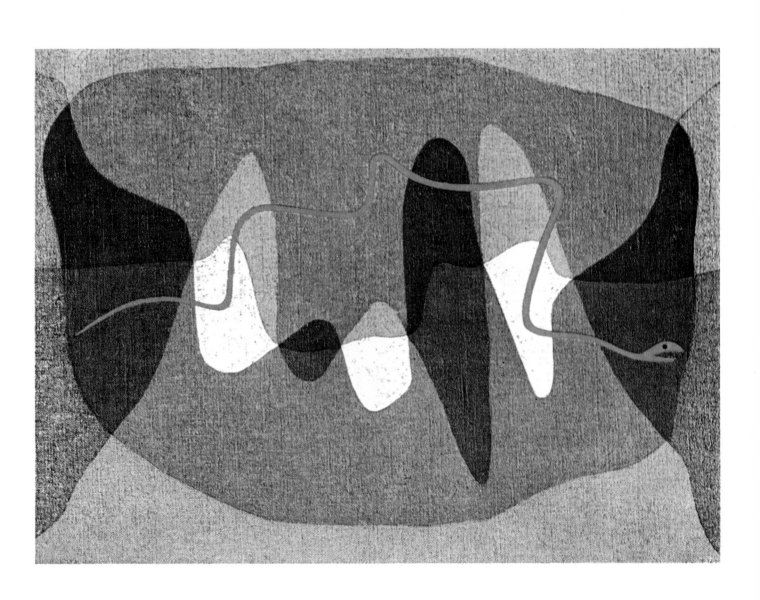

NOCTURNAL FLOWERS (Nächtliche Blumen), 1918
Aquarell, 6⅞″ × 6⅜″ (17.6 × 16.3 cm)
Folkwang Museum, Essen

and experimental forms. His signs and graphic metaphors turn to astral or, more precisely, cosmogonic illustration (*Nocturnal Flowers*, (see page 36); *Full Moon*, (see page 23)). Thus the dispersion and distribution of the planes perpetuate significant goals. Klee was aware of the difficulties involved in reading them. "The principal handicap of the person who contemplates or reproduces it [the plastic work] is that from the outset he is placed in the presence of an end result, and seemingly he can trace the path of the genesis of the work only in reverse."

At the end of 1919 he signed a three-year contract with a dealer, and major exhibitions proliferated — in Frankfurt, Hanover, Munich, and other cities. It was in this period that he stopped remounting his colored sheets. The irony, poetry, and humor of these sheets — heads, still lifes, and figures — interpenetrate indissolubly. However, as much by its characteristic signs of notation as by its equivalences of resonance, the familiar world of the senses is not absent from his calligraphy, and the parallel lines that stripe the planes of his pignouted *Angry Kaiser Wilhelm* of 1920 are reminiscent of a musical stave. When systematically developed, these horizontal and parallel lattices were later to give rise to and characterize an entire series of works.

In January 1921, in response to an invitation that had been extended the autumn before, Klee went to Weimar as a professor at the Bauhaus, which had been established several months earlier by Walter Gropius. In September his family came to join him in a spacious four-room apartment with a studio. Thus began one of the happiest and most fruitful periods of his career. It began, however, with a bereavement: the death of his mother. Perhaps as a reaction to this misfortune, some of his works, light in the center, darken toward their outer edges until they become, as it were, black borders. Moreover, Klee himself called them "mourning borders".

Despite his easily identifiable subjects, the movement toward abstraction (which in his work had first appeared in 1915 in his first works to have an architectonic substratum) is clarified and accentuated, especially in the definition of spaces (*Dream City*, see page 30, and *Picture of a Town with Red and Green Accents*, see page 21). The simultaneously experimental and methodical research extolled by the teaching staff of the Bauhaus satisfied his deep fondness for order and logic. He was very enthusiastic about his role as a teacher, and also about the fact that he was now close to his friend Kandinsky, who had returned from Moscow. He did not distinguish between his courses, which he prepared in great detail, and the research he was carrying on for his own purposes. Thus his time was divided harmoniously between creating and teaching. The geometrical surfaces of many of Klee's paintings intersect, thus creating multiple spaces, those very spaces that were soon to develop in the direction of perspective schemata. The time (1908) when he had complained that "perspective makes me yawn" was far behind him.

Around 1922 appear scenographic themes inspired by the opera and the circus, with their train of actors, accessories, and settings. Is not *The Wild Man* of that very year, with its wide-sleeved costume closed with large buttons, reminiscent of a clown? Approximately five hundred works on similar or related subjects (for example, the *Magic Theater* of 1923) were to follow. He also painted numerous works that are rhythmically and chromatically orchestrated like fugues, for he continued to "make music", as he amusingly expressed it. (Later, at Dessau, he was to "make music" much less frequently, and after his return to Bern toward the end of his life he practically stopped altogether.) In his drawings, in which a fondness for satire again overcomes him, the subject is sometimes surrounded by an entire stage setting. Certain discoveries inspired by his reading of Prinzhorn's "Plastic Activity of the Mentally Ill" were to supplement his long-standing interest in children's drawings.

He thus found confirmation of his opinion, which was not to change, that drawing is the touchstone of plastic expression. Believing that "color is the most irrational element of painting" (and perhaps feeling, without admitting, that it may also be the most essential), Klee gives priority to calligraphic formulation, which was to establish him on the path to abstraction. "It was in the nature of things that graphic art, which in itself represents an even more legitimate path toward abstraction than painting, should in our time come back into favor," he had said two years earlier, in a text published by the Blue Rider group. In his writings, in which remarks on configurations and formalities, internal schemata of the basic forms, developments of secondary forms, and irregular transformations of the basic forms abound, we find only a minimum of observations on color, its principles, and the modalities of its application. In any case, Klee did not part freely with his graphic, pencil, and ink works; he refused not only to sell them but even to show them.

In a Bauhaus anthology he published a work on "Ways of Studying Nature." Nature in his work, however, has no connection with the nature of the realistic painters, or even (despite several chance similarities) with that of the Surrealists, though it is primarily of the latter that the ever undogmatic indices of surreality or unreality, which animate his works, remind us. This is undoubtedly the source of the misunderstanding that was to affect his relations with the hard-core (notably Parisian) Surrealists. In his paintings with letters of the alphabet (*Composition with a B* and *Villa R*, both 1919, see page 22; *The Order of High C*, see page 31; *The Voice Cloth of the Singer Rosa Silber*, 1922), the use of letters had reposed less on plastic than on symbolic needs, in contrast to the Cubist use of them. These paintings had alternated with perspective studies (*Souvenir of Gersthofen*, 1918; *Room with Perspective*, 1920 and *Room Perspective with Occupants*, see page 41, in which distant echoes of Van Gogh's famous bedroom can be detected). These works were henceforth to be replaced by transparent, prismatic structures based on polyhedrons, helixes, spirals, and parallel, tangential, and secant planes. Perspective survives, to be sure, but at the same time it ceases to be representative and internal, without however becoming external, as, for example, in a work by di Chirico. Just as the numerals and letters took the place of images and words, so these planes devoid of opacity add the plausible to the fantastic and replace shadow with the limpidity of the crystal.

While the fruitfully prospective geometries of the Bauhaus were certainly not foreign to this phase of Klee's development, it is equally certain that, by virtue of the structural evidence

Monkeys Playing (Spielende Äffchen), 1919
Pen and ink, 8½″ × 7⅛″ (21.6 × 18.2 cm). Private collection, New York

that it symbolizes, the crystal had always (at least since his famous apostrophe of 1916: "Can I die, I the crystal? I the crystal?") figured as a privileged agent of fascination in the painter's personal mythology. Moreover, "crystallines" was the term by which he was to designate a series of watercolors, one of the most beautiful of which, *Graduation of the Crystal*, is today in the Basel Museum, a gift of Marguerite Arp. No hint of emotional or sensual confusion affects them, and the magic they exude, far from clouding their certainty, causes them to shine with an incomparable brilliance. By means of a composition that is perhaps intuitive in origin but is resolutely constructive in its consequences, these works illustrate the artist's statement that "sometimes the crystalline clarity of my soul was troubled, here and there, by a breath, my towers were sometimes enveloped in storm clouds," and, "in me the terrestrial makes way for the cosmic idea." At the Bauhaus, his deep-seated duality — he was neither pure poet nor pure painter — was revealed in striking fashion. Order and method were constantly being superimposed on imagination and humor (*Landscape with Yellow Birds*, see page 33 and *The Seafarer*, 1923). His works frequently originate in a complete series of observations that range from the study of formative mechanisms and morphological definitions on a preliminary diagram to the same definitions without a diagram or to hypotheses that arrange principles into a composition.

Around 1923 he adopted drawing hatchings, or stripes and screens, and painted the first "magic squares" (*Graduation of Colors from Statics to Dynamism*, 1923, followed at intervals until the end of his life, by *Rhythmical*, see page 56, *In Flower*, and others). The latter works, whose square-ruled surfaces are enlivened by several rows of small squares, can simultaneously be regarded as reminiscences of Oriental rugs or the perpetuation of a slight Cubist influence, undoubtedly a little of both. Perhaps, too, we should not underestimate the examples of Malewitch (well known to Kandinsky) and the perpendicular rhythms of Mondrian, of the same period. In the "magic squares" (kinds of hopscotch squares or grilles) the sum total of the vertical propositions would seem to equal the sum total of the horizontal propositions. This is very possible, at least for certain pieces, and would present nothing particularly disconcerting, since Klee himself was not far from conceiving of the plastic arts as a scientific discipline whose poetic substratum was based on mathematics. In any event, while the role assigned to the unconscious diminished and references to the concrete became increasingly rare in his works (except for the screens or stripes, which could have been inspired by the weaving workshops of the Bauhaus), the constructive elements became increasingly important. In other works (chiefly watercolors), in contrast, we find many sketches of plants or aquatic and solar reflections (*Cosmic Flora*, 1913, exhibited in Paris in 1948). These may be reminiscences of travels or personally experienced impressions. Although his signature appears on the work itself, the painter wrote the title assigned to the painting at the bottom, either in a margin (a kind of inner frame that seems to have been put there for that purpose) or on a passe-partout — something he had always done and almost always would do.

He took a vacation trip to Sicily, admiring that island's "pure landscape in the abstract." Klee never ceased to be hypnotized by the sun, the South, the East; with the exception of rare trips to Brittany, the Baltic Coast, or the North Sea, his spiritual compass was unfailingly

1921/24 Zimmerperspective mit Einwohnern

ROOM PERSPECTIVE WITH OCCUPANTS (Zimmerperspektive mit Einwohnern), 1921
Oil and watercolor, 19⅟₁₆″ × 12½″ (48.5 × 31.7 cm)
Paul Klee Foundation, Museum of Fine Arts, Bern

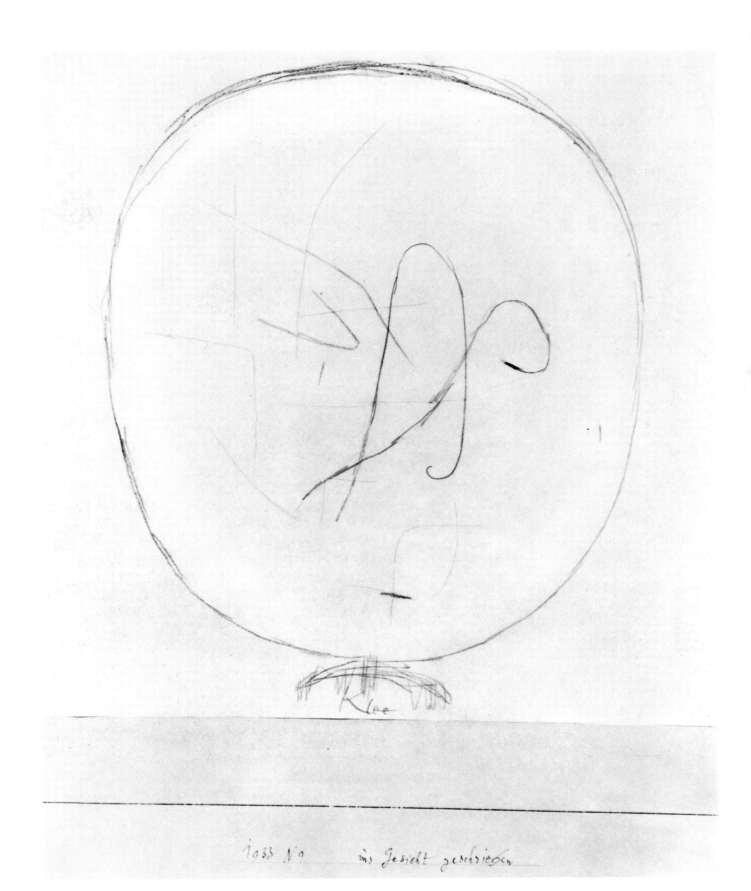

Written on the Face (Ins Gesicht geschrieben), 1933
Pencil, 12¾″ × 12¾″ (32.3 × 32.3 cm).   De Menil Collection, United States

PHYSIONOMIC LIGHTNING (Physiognomischer Blitz), 1927
Watercolor, 10″ × 10″ (25.4 × 25.4 cm).   Private collection, New York

to guide him toward the South. A short time after his return from Sicily the Weimar Bauhaus was forced to close its doors because of the hostility of the authorities. After its dissolution in Weimar, the institution was reestablished in Dessau at the beginning of 1925. It was here that his "Pedagogical Sketchbook" was published, in the Bauhausbücher series. In addition to some rather naïvely rediscovered truisms and restatements of the obvious, the "Sketchbook" contains numerous theoretical considerations on the subjective perspectives of space, modalities of composition, the relationships of measures and weights, spatial projections, and so on.

In his work of this period, the colored margins, which formed as it were a second border inside certain watercolors, disappear and fade away; the space is now continuous and is occupied by Celtic- and Runic-looking signs. In his drawings the line, whose nature is continually being modified, is sometimes drawn freehand, sometimes guided. For curves he often uses the compass, whose leadless tip also serves to engrave an intaglio line in the thickness of the paper. His technical discoveries had also been proliferating for some time past. Thus he obtained fuzzy and shaded effects within forms, effects that contrast with the precision of the outlines, thanks to a sprayer that projects the paint outside the planes protected by masks — in short, something like the system of the stencil. Klee also discovered what have been called "lace effects" — close, dense calligraphies like knitting and crochet motifs, sometimes extremely complicated and capable of being repeated *ad infinitum*, which perhaps also came about through the observation of the textiles perfected at the Bauhaus.

The direction of the hatchings (a procedure well known to engravers, who use it to indicate modeling) that accompany the lines locate the latter in space by giving them downy, mossy, or velvety aspects as desired. At first limited to the graphic works, the hatchings were soon to be integrated into Klee's watercolor vocabulary (*Carnival in the Mountains, The Bird Pep, Botanical Theater*). In this way they move from the domain of values into that of color.

Klee was a tireless visitor to the Dessau Zoo and the nearby Wörlitz Park, which was rich in exotic plants, and themes with flowers and animals became increasingly numerous in his work. Their prevalence coincides with a particularly happy period in the painter's life. Does he not remark that "the aim of a painting is, after all, to make us happy"? His delicate painted poems in a sense paraphrase the Novalis of the "Last Fragments": "The flower is the symbol of the mystery of our spirit. Would it not be possible to have a mythology of nature? — 'mythology' being understood here in my meaning: free poetic invention which symbolizes nature with great diversity." Clearly giving expression to the innocent, one could almost say the Franciscan, and very moving side of his spirit, Klee was later to say: "One can rediscover oneself in the plant. Just as St. Francis called all creatures 'sister'..." (quoted by Petra Petitpierre). In any case, there is no doubt that this flora and fauna of Wörlitz, which he so carefully and lovingly observed, had infinitely more repercussions on the flowering of his expression than did that Zoroastrian Mazdaism to which, somewhat ingenuously, some of his Bauhaus colleagues offered sacrifices. His art partakes of a kind of animism quite similar to

BLACK PRINCE (Schwarzer Fürst), 1927
Oil, 13″ × 11⅞₁₆″ (33 × 29 cm). Kunstsammlung Nordrhein-Westfalen, Düsseldorf

SHIPS SETTING SAIL (Abfahrt der Schiffe), 1927
Oil, 19¹¹⁄₁₆″ × 23⅝″ (50 × 60 cm)
Private collection, Bern

STILL LIFE WITH PLANT AND WINDOW
(Pflanze und Fenster Stilleben), 1927
Oil, watercolor, and gouache, 18$^{11}\!/_{16}$" × 23" (47.5 × 58.5 cm)
Collection Ernst Beyeler, Basel

Figurine "The Old Woman" (Figurine die Alte), 1927
Oil, 15¾″ × 12³⁄₁₆″ (40 × 31 cm). Marlborough Fine Art Ltd., London

that of the child and the primitive, and against a background of pantheism breathes a spiritual life into every substance, inert and otherwise — stones, fish, birds.

While composition with parallel lines and repetitions and alternances with rhythmic devolution were developing, however, the mysterious and the nocturnal (in *Ships Setting Sail,* for example, see page 46), like plastic echoes of oneiric apparitions, were occupying another broad sector of his production. Thus, in Paris, on the occasion of Klee's first one-man showing at the Galerie Vavin-Raspail, René Crevel wrote, "I have become acquainted with animals of soul, birds of intelligence, fish of heart, and plants with dream." In order to diversify his spaces and their specific ambiences, the painter multiplies his vanishing lines, for the last-mentioned, above and beyond the geometric Euclidean logic, are aimed above all at psychological impact.

In Klee's works, then, the greater the precision seems to be, the more sonorous are the reverberations of his unreality of interpretation. Like diagrams, his transpositions, devoid of the fantastication of inspiration, and his ghostly schemata, at once absurd and transparent, exist in a rarefied atmosphere. Scattered over the surface, but a function of the exact space they occupy, the hieroglyphs invented by the artist (*Abstract Script*, a drawing of 1931, of *New Secret Script*, a gouache of 1935) transcend the simple illustrative role of occupation of the plane and, incantatory or conjurational, accede to the virtues of genuine plastic magic (*Around the Fish; Black Prince*, see page 45).

He went to Italy again during the summer of 1926. In additon to the Uffizi at Florence, he was delighted by the mosaics at Ravenna; according to Felix Klee, through their textural aspects they were to influence a sector of his future work, which is highly probable. In 1927 he went to Corsica, from which he brought back little, it seems, but a certain lightening of tonalities. The character of his works of this period, less fairylike than that of the works he created at Weimar but in which the imaginary holds an equally large place, may instead be hallucinatory. Compositions with straight or curved parallel lines, a continuation of the earlier musical staves, followed in succession. In 1929 he made his copper engraving *Old Man Reckoning.* His graphic experiments, very numerous at this time, are not necessarily integrated into painting; they seem to be self-sufficient. This line, melodiously continuous like the flow of the tide, or broken up into scattered sections, now express the progression of rhythmic ideas. His line becomes a lattice, a net, a mesh, fringes, image-and-idea traps in which the was and the becoming are dissolved. Like a child in his games imitating an adult, he reproduces in his speech the play of the forces "that created and create the world".

At the Bauhaus the internal condition of the establishment was evolving rapidly during this period, and Klee imperceptibly moved from full adherence to reserve. Gropius had resigned from the directorship, and the responsibility was now in the hands of the Swiss architect Hannes Meyer. Moreover, the artist was already growing weary, not of teaching in itself but of its restrictive aspect, and his weariness did not disappear with the departure of Meyer and his replacement in 1930 by Mies van der Rohe.

In the winter of 1928-1929 there occurred the third decisive trip in Paul Klee's life, this one to Egypt. Like his earlier travels in Italy and Tunisia, this voyage was to accelerate and precipitate the movement of his intellectual and plastic development. Before the grandiose remains of a fabulous past he had a presentiment of the unity of life and eternity, the ephemeral and the perpetual. His on-the-spot sketches are symbioses of his individual, contemporary, and specific existence and of bygone ages — atavism and modernity, so to speak. This is the source of those manifestations of an intermediate state that is neither completely life nor completely death, but beyond the phenomenon of birth, another aspect of neutrality.

He returns repeatedly, in the course of several decades to this idea ("...and the best would be not to be born"), which he clarifies ("In me there circulates the blood of a better age. I wander through the present century like a sleepwalker, I remain attached to the old homeland, to the tomb of my native land.For everything was swallowed up by the ground"), repeats ("...can I have gotten lost inside myself? In this case it would have been better never to have been born"), enlarges into a command, a piece of advice, or an invitation ("Imagine that you are dead..."), expresses in verse ("I am armed, I am not of this place / I am in the abyss, I am far away... / I am burning among the dead"), improves on for greater precision ("My ardor belongs more to the order of the dead and unborn creatures"), and finally has engraved as an epitaph on his tombstone in the little cemetery at Schlosshalden ("I cannot be understood in purely earthly terms, for I can live as happily with the dead as with the unborn; somewhat nearer to the heart of all creation than is usual, but still far from being near enough").

The signs of his cosmogony, a kind of pictorial stenography, increase in number. The arrows, directional signs, and the moons of his adolescence ("The moon was a pearl which actually signified tears") and Tunis ("As for me, however, I am the rising Southern moon") were now joined by the sun of Cairo and Alexandria with its "dark power." Without modeling, "trompe-l'œil", chiaroscuro or classic perspective, thanks solely to the eurythmics of his luminous geometries, he solves the problem of plastic space, depth adhering to the plane of the painting. He seems, moreover, to have premonitions of these geometries in 1925, as if he already bore within himself, unknown to his conscious and buried in the folds of a remembering clairvoyance, the seed of his future discoveries. In this way he transcends, through the effects of a mental dialectic that is less conciliatory than symbiotic, the opposition and conflicts that were rending contemporary European art. Moreover, on the level of pictorial development this same dialectic had long been maintaining the cohesion of the component formal elements scattered over the surface. In addition it was now coordinating the movements of these elements within spaces that seem endowed with elasticity. In a few years the spaces themselves would be occupied by distended surfaces and dynamic spatial elements. For the moment, it was elasticity that distinguished his latest expression of extension from his Cézannean interpretations of Tunis and the para-Cubist expression of the war years. In the order of priorities that the painter was now following, rhythm having to a certain extent supplanted form, the figurations with planes striped with parallel lines, which utilized the environment like a musical background, become landscapes by way of colored strips (they look like fields viewed from an airplane) endowed with a total unity of construction.

The Steamer Passes the Botanical Garden
(Der Dampfer Fährt am Botanischen Garten Vorbei), 1921
India ink, 4¾" × 11⅜" (12 × 28.8 cm)
Paul Klee Foundation, Museum of Fine Arts, Bern

Catastrophe I Four (Katastrophe I Vier), 1925
China ink, 7¼" × 9¼" (18.4 × 23.5 cm)
Saidenberg Gallery, New York

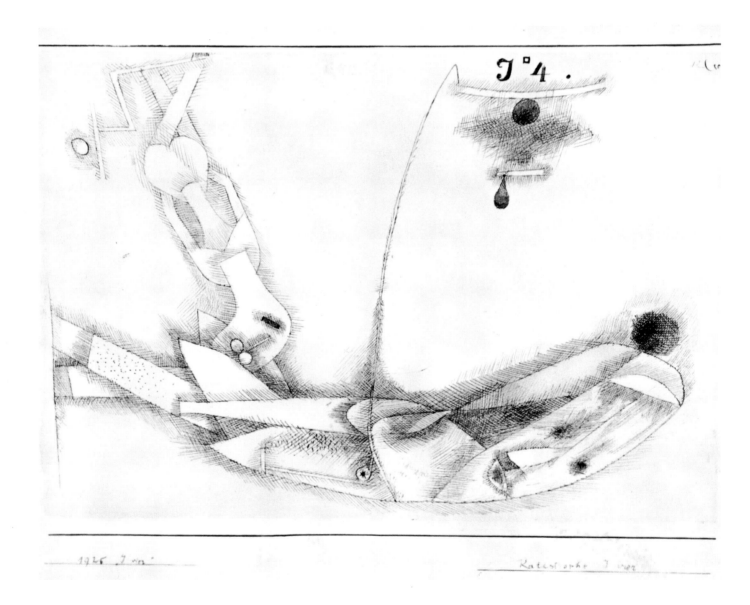

Plummets to the Wave (Lote zur Welle), 1928
Oil, 19¼″ × 27½″ (48.8 × 69.8 cm)
Saidenberg Gallery, New York

Still Life (Stilleben), 1938
Detail. Collection Felix Klee, Bern

BROTHER AND SISTER (Geschwister), 1930
Oil and watercolor, 27⅞″ × 17¾″ (70.7 × 45.2 cm).   Collection Jan Krugier, Geneva

RHYTHMICAL (Rythmisches), 1930
Oil, 27⅛″ × 19⅝″ 69.6 × 50.5 cm). Musée National d'Art Moderne, Centre Georges Pompidou, Paris

Klee visited Gizeh, Luxor, the Valley of the Kings, Aswan and its temples, as well as the Roman ruins of Sicily, where he made a stopover on his way home. Back in Europe and Dessau, Klee exploited the rich harvest brought back from his journey. We now observe two series of works: one in which the spatial continuum is assured practically without chromatism and another, of more lyrical works in which the atmospheric composition opens out into the interior space. We also note repeatedly the permanence of the prismatic structures through the multiple facets of which the volumes are expressed (*Tale*, 1929; *Castle Hill*, 1929; *At Seven above the Roofs*, 1930; *Floating Town*, see page 63; *Kettledrum Organ*, 1930), the continuation of composition with parallel lines (*Boat Approaching the Shore*, 1929; *Monument in Fertile Country*, 1930), and the persistence of transformations (*Hovering, Before the Ascent*). This coexistence in time of completely different manners and styles — an interval of one year separates *Brother and Sister* (see page 55) and *Doorway of a Mosque* — demonstrates that just as it is impossible to confine Klee within historical and esthetic categories independent of him without betraying him, neither can we understand his extraordinarily multidirectional work if we arbitrarily divide his plastic evolution into chronological or other periods.

In 1930 the painter introduced the denominations that he was henceforth to use in classifying his output. His drawings, watercolors, and paintings now became panel pictures, colored sheets, and paintings. In the case of mixed techniques this classification obviously lent itself to a good deal of confusion and ambiguity. He was studying the possibilities of mobility offered by the arrangement of several components on their background; sometimes, too, his surfaces seemed to stretch. In addition, he now painted a series of pictures (*Diana; Light and So Much Else; At Anchor*) in which color, laid on in tiny, isolated strokes like a scattering of seeds, punctuates his planes. He was to call these paintings "Divisionist," although to tell the truth the technique of their effects relates them more closely to a simple process of surface occupation than to the Pointillism of Luce and Signac or to the genuine Division of Seurat, with its chromatism that was at once pictorial and scientific. The stroke and the line, those purely cerebral, antinatural methods of expression, which are the only real constants in Klee's painting and which he could not do without, are always present. Through them, and by playing like a virtuoso on all the registers of the keyboard they offer him, the artist achieves space and light, a space and light that moreover are essentially poetic, being in turn crystalline, as if made of ice, or as warm as popular legend. He now abandoned the spraying method, and although it was still his desire that color should in no way weaken his drawing, he made it less subordinate than in the preceding year to the signs, arrows, crosses, circles, stars, and so on, which are slightly tranformed and fall into outlines that at times could almost be Gaelic. From the anecdote to the symbol, inspiration thus passes directly into language.

In April 1931, Klee gave up his contract with the Bauhaus, which, now at Dessau, had only three semesters longer to live. (Later, after an unsuccessful attempt had been made to continue it in Berlin, it was to be completely abolished.) That year the painter returned to Sicily, where he visited the archaeological sites. With its subdued harmonies, interlaced script, and plastic ornamentality, Klee's art is sometimes reminiscent of the archaic expression of primitive societies.

Sternly Physiognomic (Physiognomisch streng), 1930
Pencil, 16″ × 10½″ (40.6 × 26.7 cm).   Collection Maurine and Robert Rothschild, New York

The Yellow Girl (Ohne Titel), 1919
Watercolor, 12½" × 9¼" (31.7 × 23.5 cm). Private collection

It seems to be the product of a synthesis of imaginary ethnologies and actual interpreted documents, rugs, mosaics, inscriptions, fabrics, and so on.

In Düsseldorf, where he was a part-time teacher at the Academy of Fine Arts from 1931 to 1933, Klee simultaneously satisfied his need to be surrounded by young people and his desire to have more free time for himself. In the "Paris of the Rhineland," as Düsseldorf was commonly called, he painted small pointillist oils, vaguely Neo-Impressionist in style (*Plant Tendril; Through a Window; Cliff by the Sea; Barbarian Sacrifice*), in accordance with a system of speckling that we find already in use in earlier drawings, notably drawings dating from 1925 (*Portrait of Dr. G.* and *Sweet*).

Although the memory of his travels was fading, despite frequent consultation of the sketchbooks he had brought back, we note, through the systematic distribution of the planes, the persistence of his Egyptian impressions (*Arab Song*, see page 71). Nevertheless, it is the works originating from within that now predominate (*Fire at Full Moon*, see page 73), with their thematic deepening of the formal element to the point of occultation. In Düsseldorf he also did several oils characterized by thick masses of pigment, including *The Future Man*, which with its grids and textures is much more reminiscent than the divisionist works of the mosaics of Ravenna, and which seems to herald the development of the *Angels* series of 1939.

However, the time of troubles was now at hand. Insults and official attacks on modern art, and on his art in particular, were becoming increasingly virulent. He was frequently accused of being a Jew and a "foreigner"; with great nobility, he refrained from defending himself against the charge. After a trip to France, just before Christmas of 1933, Klee took the road to exile in Switzerland and Bern, the city of his childhood, while Kandinsky decided to settle in Paris.

Paul Klee was now, at the age of fifty-four, an artist of world renown. He had exhibited in the largest museums and galleries, not only in Germany and Switzerland but also in the United States, France, Belgium, and England — and this despite the fact that, as André Masson was to comment in 1946, his work "remains under the seal of secrecy. Thus it stands in its proper place, in the carefully concealed order of spiritual values." However, this did not prevent his ungrateful country from putting up for sale 102 of his works, arbitrarily and illegally sequestered, on the occasion of the "Degenerate Art" exhibition in Munich four years later. Perhaps it was the anxieties consequent upon his emigration that interrupted the production of his very beautiful pastels, with their harmonies of a rare luminous brilliance, and drove him to resume or complete earlier themes (among other things he finished the *Botanical Theater*, begun ten years earlier), as well as to pursue already cultivated modes of expression such as *The Soul Departs*, reminiscent of Egyptian embalming techniques, or *Mountain Village* (see page 70), constructed like a puzzle. His hieroglyphic scripts are secret conventions by which he expresses simultaneously his quality of a visionary dwelling outside of time and his keen sense of modernity. The first stage of this Bernese period was a kind of withdrawal into gains won earlier. It was succeeded by watercolors in which an ideal light spreads over the skin of natural

A Crusader (Ein Kreuzfahrer), 1929
Watercolor, 18″ × 11¼″ (45.7 × 28.6 cm). Private collection, New York

House of the Firm Z (Haus der Firma Z), 1922
Watercolor, 11¼" × 8½" (28.5 × 21.5 cm). Private collection, New York

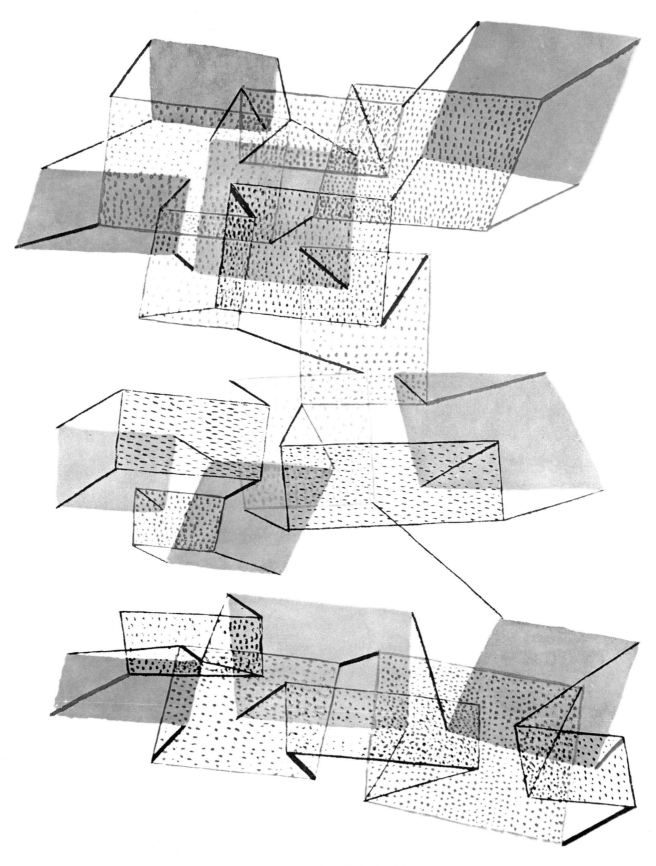

FLOATING TOWN (Segelnde Stadt), 1930
Watercolor, 19⁹⁄₁₆″ × 14⁹⁄₁₆″ (49 × 37 cm).   Private collection

components, that is, components known through experience but consciously transposed and combined with the pictorial expression.   The harmony of the color areas along their dividing lines in generally assured sometimes by their equality of luminous intensity, sometimes by the common element of their complementary nature or by their warm-cool relationships.   Thus they are either broken and of equal values, or of unequal but complementary values.   (The use in their pure state of primary colors of unequal value remains rare).

During the summer of 1935, as a result of bronchial, pulmonary, and cardiac complications resulting from measles, Klee was attacked by the first symptoms of a little-known disease called scleroderma, the drying out of the skin and the mucous membranes, which five years later was to be the cause of his death.   Within the plastic expression of anxiety, clearly indicated

Park beside a Lake (Park am See), 1920
Wash, 6″ × 8¾″ (15.2 × 22.2 cm).   Private collection, New York

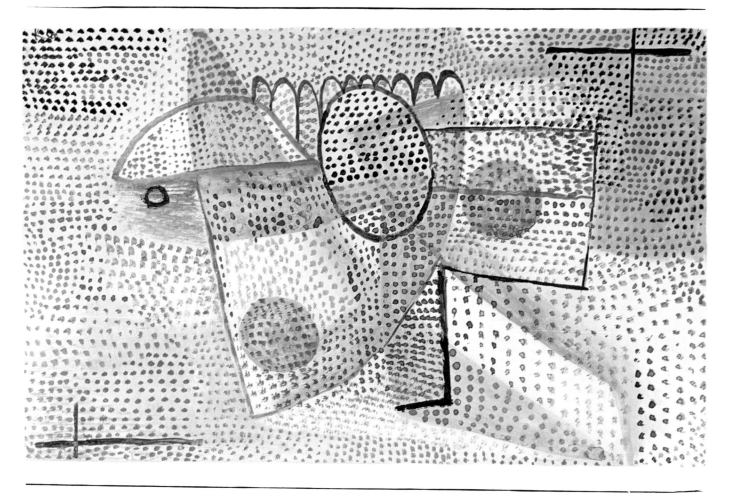

1931 N 20   Schlir-Stilleben

"SCHLIR" STILL LIFE (Schlir-Stilleben), 1931
Watercolor, 8¼" × 12⅞" (21 × 32.6 cm)
Marlborough Gallery, New York

Demonry (Daemonie), 1925
China ink, 9⅞″ × 21¾″ (25.1 × 55.4 cm). Paul Klee Foundation, Museum of Fine Arts, Bern

by his titles (*Destroyed Country*, 1934; *Diagram of Redemption*, 1934; *Growing Weapons, 1935; Proud Defense*, 1935), Klee pushes back the limits of intelligibility and communication by the irrefragability of his topologies like so many genuine geometries of situations.

Klee spent the major part of 1936 taking cures. Although it was a year of scanty production for the artist, it seems nonetheless to have paved the way for the magnificent burst of creativity, similar to an apotheosis, of the second Bernese period. The color, on the burst planes of sundered forms, is harmonized in dominants that are either cool (*Figure in a Garden*) or warm (*Stage Landscape*). This is also the great period of his pastels, among the best of which is his *Oriental Garden* (see page 81). The decomposition that he inflicts on his forms endows the resulting components with a character of liberation and explosion which, while certainly not joyous is full of life (*Harmonized Combat*, see page 83). We recognize, one would say in rejuvenated form, several of his favorite subjects — the theater, the East, music — sometimes combined with other subjects, such as the eye, all outlined by means of an insistent script which is broad and black. Frequently this script, with a halo of light along its edges, seems to radiate its own light (*Red Waistcoat; Park Beside a Lake*, see page 64; *The Vase*). At least the seriousness of life (*Strokes from Heroic Bows*, see page 85, with its variant, *The Gray Man and the Coastline*, both dating from 1938, and *Revolution of the Viaduct*), if not its violence, is generally implied in these works. Along with crayon drawings, pastels on cloth, and waxed

66

watercolors treated with oil or water (or a combination of both), appear the large works, done more to satisfy a need for intensity than to promote a monumental diction. These are figures, heads, and landscapes, and their expression is of such simplicity that it masks, apparently without effort, the complexity of their components.

The *Broken Key* in a sense inaugurates the final dramatic phase of the painter's language. The struggle between limited, closed forms and free, open forms is already taking shape in this language. Klee's art now becomes an adventure in constant process of renewal. In 1939, perhaps with a presentiment of his approaching death, Klee increased his output, constantly widening the area of his investigations and experiments. Having completed the cycle *Everything That Stands on Its Feet Walks and Runs*, he began the *Approaches, Eidola, Infernal Park, Angels,* and *Ourx* cycles.

Classical East-Coast Landscape (Ost-Klassiche Küstenlandschaft), 1936
Pen and ink, 13″ × 18⅞″ (33.1 × 48 cm). Paul Klee Foundation, Museum of Fine Arts, Bern

SMALL TOWN AMONG THE ROCKS (Kleine Felsenstadt), 1932
Oil, 17⅝″ × 22¹⁄₁₆″ (44 × 56 cm)
Paul Klee Foundation, Museum of Fine Arts, Bern

68

Thus he entered the third and final period of his earthly life. The humor that "should enable us to overcome all things" was still alive in him, to be sure, but it darkened and became black, like his earth-colored, ash-gray palette stamped with what he had once recommended: "Fortunate is the artist who plants his figurative accessory on the spot where a last tiny hole remains, and where it looks as if it had belonged from all eternity." His charcoal then seeks and gropes over the spot that "still presents a slight formal insufficiency." This was not a "trick of the trade," a formula, or a camouflage of insufficiency, as some might believe, but a conscious and beneficient use of the "slips" that occur in every genesis, a mutation of the defect into a quality, by virtue of the principle that none of the possibilities opened to the artist by the accidents, good and bad, of the formulation are to be neglected. Thus his exactly adequate methods of expression are adapted to his vision. For one who knows how to hear, these methods, allusive and simplified to an extreme degree, are a celebration of farce in the key of tragedy. Moreover, the demons, frequent apparitions in his work — for they were always part of his secret world: "The diabolical shows the tip of an ear here and there, and cannot be repressed" — reappear in large numbers. In Klee's art, which is evocative if not exorcistic and which ultimately seems to act merely as a medium, they surge up from the painter's unconscious to the surface of the picture. Earlier, speaking of the creative act and its responsibility, he had already noted that "the evolution of a work of art causes [it] to be consummated in the subconscious."

Together with the Angels, who bear a strange resemblance to them, the Demons represent the creatures of a world that is at once outside of and anterior to our own. Nonarchetypal in their inspiration like the cosmic vocabulary of an earlier period, and barely Manichaean in their formulation, both combine grace of formal vehicle with monstrous content. "The diabolical will dissolve into the celestial, dualism will not be treated as such but as its contradictory truth." In them, and in their representation of creatures that can be conceived only by the imagination, divergences are resolved, distinctions are reunited, the oppositions between beauty and ugliness, dream and reality, life and death are abolished. "The work of Paul Klee," René Crevel wrote at about this time, "is a complete museum of the dream." Around 1939 the artist's expression, without exaggerated pathos, was nevertheless sliding faster in the direction of the morbid, a kind of anguish.

Then came a brief interruption in this evolution of the plastic message, in the form of several rigorously constructed pictures whose surface are completely compartmented: *Double and Newly Arranged Place*, both dating from 1940. The titles Klee assigned his works, although still as enigmatically poetic as before, corroborate his gloomy frame of mind: *Destroyed Labyrinth; Pathetic Germination; Sick Man in a Boat; Dark Navigation*. The themes of the ship, the sea, and the boat-crossing, which like that of the voyage are the mythical representations of life itself, had not disappeared from his psychological motivations. Klee, adjusted to his circumstances, was merely diverted toward the pessimistic horizons ruled over by fate. In a letter to Will Grohmann, quoted by Grohmann in his monumental work on the painter, several months before his death, Klee wrote: "Naturally I have not struck the tragic vein without some preparation. Many of my works point the way with their message: The time has come."

Mountain Village in Autumn (Bergdorf herbstlich), 1934
Oil, 28⅛″ × 21⅜″ (71.5 × 54.4 cm).   Collection S. Rosengart, Lucerne

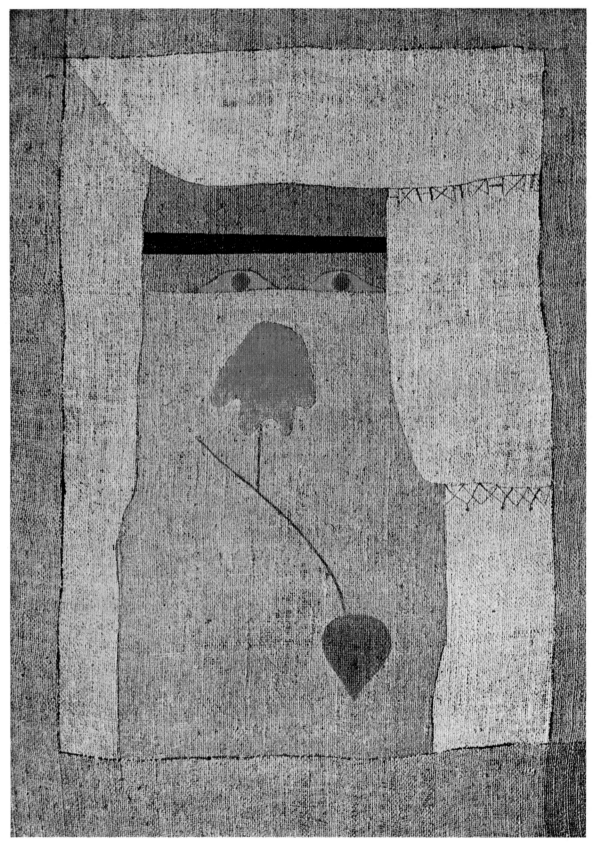

ARAB SONG (Arabisches Lied), 1932
Gouache, 35¾″ × 25⅛″ (96 × 64 cm).   The Phillips Gallery, Washington, D.C.

AD PARNASSUM, 1932
Oil, 39⅜″ × 49⅝″ (100 × 126 cm)
Museum of Fine Arts, Bern

Fire at Full Moon (Feuer bei Vollmond), 1933
Watercolor and wax, 19¹¹⁄₁₆″ × 23⅝″ (50 × 60 cm)
Folkwang Museum, Essen

INFLUENCE (Influenz), 1932
Gouache, 12¼″ × 19½″ (31 × 49.5 cm)
Marlborough Gallery, New York

FRIENDLY GAME (Freundliches Spiel), 1933
Watercolor, 10⅝″ × 11¹³⁄₁₆″ (27 × 30 cm)
Former Huggler collection, Bern

To Escape (Entfliegen), 1934
Watercolor, 13⅜″ × 19⅛″ (34 × 48.5 cm)
Saidenberg Gallery, New York

City of Lagoons (Lagunenstadt), 1927
India ink, 11¹⁵⁄₁₆″ × 18³⁄₁₆″ (30.3 × 46.3 cm)
Paul Klee Foundation, Museum of Fine Arts, Bern

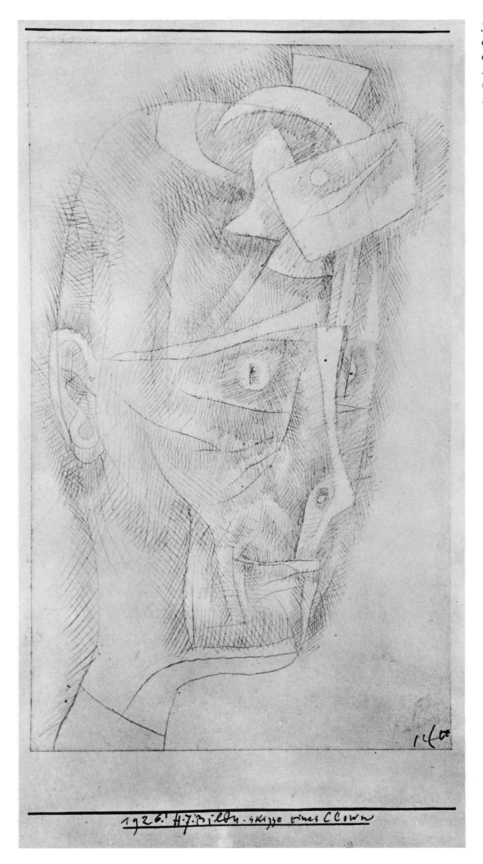

1926. H. 7. Bilder-skizze eines Clown

Sketch Portrait
of a Clown (Bilder-skizze
eines Clown) 1926
Pencil, 8¼" × 4¾"
(21 × 12 cm)
Private collection

Combed or Disheveled?
(Frisur oder Strubel?), 1939
Watercolor, 8¼″ × 3¼″ (21 × 8.2 cm)
Private collection, New York

Shopgirl and Customer (Ladnerin und Kundin), 1937
Tempera, 10¹/₁₆″ × 19³/₁₆″ (25.6 × 49.8 cm).   Paul Klee Foundation, Museum of Fine Arts, Bern

In addition to bringing the return of those thick, black bars or strokes, so much like the leading of stained-glass windows and which, by the feeling that seeems to have dictated them, are reminiscent of the "mourning borders" at the time of his mother's death some twenty years earlier, the premonition of the ineluctable also causes a continuation of the conflict of the forms that struggle to maintain their internal homogeneity.   Where does victory lie?   In the enclosure of their planes, firmly emplaced under the protection of their intact contours?   Or in the liberating combustion, rich in a new, autonomous life, which is to disperse them to the four corners of the picture?   For these paintings he adopted coarse canvases, often prepared with stucco according to a method with which he had very often experimented, rough-surfaced papers, and granular, rough cardboard, which his palette, by turns matt or luminous (one could think it was phosphorescent), was to enliven with broadly modulated areas of color.   He also painted relatively large (at least for him) pictures in which the bodies of the figures, in contrast to the consistency they retain in the drawings, lose their bulk (*Kettledrum Player; Dancer*). Except for their heads they are like skeletons, very schematic silhouettes, almost bare bones, and by its power and authority their style combines volume with simplification.

A veritable explosion of his creative genius increased Klee's powers (or what remained of them, for his health did not improve at all) tenfold.   He drew and painted without stopping, with

ORIENTAL GARDEN (Garten im Orient), 1937
Pastel, 14¼″ × 11⅛″ (36.3 × 28.2 cm)
Collection Mr. and Mrs. James W. Alsdorf, Winnetka, Illinois

1937 / 7

Klee

BLUE-BIRD-SQUASH (Blau-Vogel-Kürbis), 1939
Gouache, 11″ × 16⅞″ (28 × 43 cm)
Collection Heinz Berggruen, Paris

HARMONIZED COMBAT (Harmonisierter Kampf), 1937
Pastel, 22⅜″ × 33¹³⁄₁₆″ (57 × 86 cm)
Paul Klee Foundation, Museum of Fine Arts, Bern

Funeral Procession (Im Trauerzug), 1939
Pencil, 8³⁄₁₆″ × 11¹¹⁄₁₆″ (20.9 × 29.7 cm)
Paul Klee Foundation, Museum of Fine Arts, Bern

STROKES FROM HEROIC BOWS (Heroische Bogenstriche), 1938
Thick tempera on newsprint, 28¾″ × 20¾″ (73 × 52.7 cm).   Museum of Modern Art, New York

LOFTY WATCHMAN (Hoher Wächter), 1949
Waxcolor, 27⁹⁄₁₆″ × 19¹¹⁄₁₆″ (70 × 50 cm).   Paul Klee Foundation, Museum of Fine Arts, Bern

STILL LIFE (Stilleben), 1938
Oil, 39⅜″ × 31½″ (100 × 80 cm).   Collection Felix Klee, Bern

CAPTIVE (Gefangen), 1940 (not catalogued)
Oil, 18⅞″ × 17⅜″ (48 × 44.2 cm).   Private collection, New York

frenzy, as if in the grip of an irresistible haste. He painted barred structures or grilles, cages of a sort (*Captive; Wood House in Enclosure*, symbolic signs that are varieties of ideograms of an exemplary sobriety of calligraphy (*Wounded Man; Locksmith; Sailor*, and its other version, *Lofty Watchman*, see page 86), and finally his last painting, *Still Life*, which, compositionally speaking, is strangely calmed by the serene equilibrium of the colored masses despite the dramatic nature of certain motifs.

At the same time, once the apocalyptic series of the *Angels* was finished, he had expressed his horror of the sufferings inflicted on humanity in some ten sheets entitled *The Passion in Detail*. Then came his last gouaches and drawings, the *Ourx* series, a kind of fantastic bestiary in which an imaginary animal with horns and heavy jowls, half bull and half bear (*ours*) (perhaps a variant of the Bernese bear?) expresses the brute force and savage, primitive violence that have suddenly loomed up out of the night of time in the middle of the modern age. Like the *Angels*, whose delineation in a synthetic, dynamic line sanctions their plausibility, there are imaginary creatures through whom Paul Klee, who felt "yesterday and today as a simultaneity," reintegrated the past into the present in a single eternity. ("...Life rustled like a springtime while crossing the centuries," wrote Novalis in his "Hymns to Night".) Thus time completely loses its transitory, circumstantial character, for the intermediate zone of the "unborn beings" in which this monstrous, vaguely anthropomorphic fauna develops, is situated as much on the level of an imaginary memory as on that of a remembering imagination. One imagines a kind of modern Hieronymus Bosch who would accumulate plastic and thematic inventions.

Although its creator may have wanted this monster to be neutral (for since he fuses Good and Evil he is not taking sides), it is nevertheless a piece of testimony, an accusation. To be sure, in the works painted toward the end of his life, man tends to disappear, to the benefit of disturbing or bizarre creatures that are abnormally shaped by way of excess or shortage; and to be sure, he always regarded himself as less a human being than "a cosmic point." A distance nevertheless seems to be established between the artist and his depictions. While at a given moment he had become by identification, as suggested by one of his masters, "flower, animal, poetry, star," now he was very certainly neither the people of the *Infernal Park* nor an *Ourx*. In addition, his demiurgic impartiality and his neutrality were never applied indiscriminately in every situation, for he had frequently expressed the wish "...to perform an action... as a unit here on earth in relation with the beyond."

Using a minimum of plastic media, but with an exact knowledge of the compositional properties peculiar to each, which made all doctrine of composition superfluous, his forms tend toward the highest precision. Their modulated calligraphy now ductile and unfettered, now authoritarian, is truly all-sufficing, thus achieving, by means of the release of several phantasms by which his "self" escapes from the restraining grip of reality and its contingencies, the artist's long-standing ambition to "reassemble" the line and to "intercept the impressionist vacillation." Fourteen years earlier that calligraphy had by its spontaneity, primitiveness, skillful absence of constraint, power of evocation, and, in a word, genuine "openness" confirmed the words

Rejected (Hinabgestossen), 1939
Chalk, 8¼″ × 11⅝″ (20.9 × 29.7 cm)
Paul Klee Foundation, Museum of Fine Arts, Bern

Sea Landscape with Heavenly Body (Seelandschaft m. d. Himmelkörper), 1920
India ink, 5″ × 11″ (12.7 × 28.1 cm). Paul Klee Foundation, Museum of Fine Arts, Bern

of Henri Michaux: "A line dreams. Until then a line had never been allowed to dream. A line hopes. A line thinks again of a face."

Whether through carelessness on his part or that of the authorities, Paul Klee, a German citizen who had resided abroad for several years, waited some time before receiving an affirmative reply to his request for a Swiss residence permit. To this delay was added, undoubtedly because of the war, a delay in the consideration of his later request for Swiss naturalization. This explains, if it does not excuse, the fact that the favorable answer of the authorities came not to him during his lifetime but to his relatives a short time after his death.

In the spring of 1940 the poor condition of his health further deteriorated, and he was taken to a hospital in Locarno. Fifty days later, on June 29, 1940, in the presence of his wife, his friends, and the helpless doctors, and a few months after his father's death, the man who in the powerful phrase of Tristan Tzara had give his contemporaries "a birth-of-the-world cure" joined in the reaches of the other world the creatures that he had wrung from it for our benefit and into which his art had been able to breathe a life more authentic and durable than that of his century.

BIOGRAPHY

1879   On December 18, Paul Klee is born at Münchenbuchsee, near Bern, to a German father and a half-French, half-Swiss mother, both musicians. He has a sister, Mathilde, born in 1876.

1880   The Klee family moves to Bern; after moving several times, finally settles permanently in a house at Obstbergweg 6.

1885   Paul's maternal grandmother teaches him to use pastels.

1886   Starts primary school; begins study of the violin.

1890-1898   Junior-high-school and high-school studies; is a mediocre student, but enthusiastic about the study of Greek. Forms friendships with Fritz Lotmar, the future brain specialist, and Hans Bloesch. Joins the Symphony Orchestra of Bern as a supernumerary; plays Bach and Mozart. Writes several short stories and poems. Vacations and excursions around the Lake of Thun, Saint Beatenberg (where his maternal aunt Louise manages a hotel-restaurant), Fribourg, etc.

1898   Receives his high-school diploma. Leaves for Munich to study painting. On the advice of Ludwig Löfftz, Director of the Academy of Fine Arts, joins Heinrich Knirr's preparatory class.

1899   Makes the acquaintance of Lily Stumpf (b. 1876), daughter of a Munich doctor.

1900   Is accepted into Stuck's class at the Academy. Also begins the study of engraving. Does a few sculptures.

1901   First trip for study purposes: Italy, in the company of the Swiss sculptor Hermann Haller. Visits Milan, Genoa, Leghorn, Pisa, Rome. Becomes engaged to Lily.

1902   Visits Naples, Rome, Florence. After eight months in Italy, returns to his parents' home in Bern.

1903   First etchings.

1905   First trip to Paris, with Louis Moilliet and Hans Bloesch. Visits the museums (Leonardo, Goya, Tintoretto, Watteau, Chardin) and attends concerts. Sees little of modern art. Back in Bern, experiments with glass-painting.

1906   Rapid visit to Berlin to see works by Leibl, Trübner, Menzel, and to Karlsruhe, where he sees the work of Grünewald. In Bern, studies Goya, Toulouse-Lautrec, Munch. Two of his engravings are accepted for the Munich "Sezession" exhibition. In September, marries Lily; in October they settle in Munich, at Ainmillerstrasse 32.

1907   Visits exhibitions of the Impressionists and a Toulouse-Lautrec retrospective. His submissions are rejected by the "Sezession" jury. Through Ernst Sonderegger, discovers the work of Ensor and Honoré Daumier. On November 30, birth of his son, Felix Klee.

1908   Visits two Van Gogh exhibitions and reads Van Gogh's correspondence with his brother Theo.

1909   Admires eight paintings by Cézanne at the "Sezession" exhibition. Several works are exhibited in Berlin.

1910   Museum at Bern, Zurich, and Winterthur exhibits fifty-five of his recent works.

1911   The same exhibition arrives at the Basel Museum. Kubin comes to visit him in Munich, where he exhibits works in the corridor of the Tannhäuser Gallery. Participates in the establishment of the *Sema* group, with Kaspar, Kubin, and Scharff. First illustration for Voltaire's "Candide." Becomes acquainted with Franz Marc, August Macke, Vassily Kandinsky, Marianne von Werefkin, Alexis Jawlensky,

Campendonck, Gabriele Münter, and Arp. Travels in Switzerland. Exhibits with the Blue Rider group in Munich, where he notices the Douanier Rousseau and Delaunay.

1912   Second visit to Paris. Becomes acquainted with Le Fauconnier and Delaunay. Sees canvases by Braque and Picasso at Wilhelm Uhde's gallery. Participates in the Blue Rider exhibition at the Goltz Gallery in Munich. Publishes an article about an exhibition in Zurich in the periodical "Die Alpen."

1913   Translates a text of Delaunay for the periodical "Der Sturm." Exhibits in the Sturm Gallery in Berlin.

1914   Second of his three major trips: Tunisia, which he visits in company of Macke and Moilliet. Paints a series of watercolors of Kairoyan, Saint-Germain, Hammamet, etc. Returns home by way of Sicily and Italy. World War I breaks out; his Russian friends leave Germany. On September 16 Macke is killed during Joffre's counteroffensive.

1915   Klee is visited by Rainer Maria Rilke.

1916   Marc is killed at Verdun. Klee is drafted into the reserves and is sent to Landshut, Munich, Schleissheim, and then Gersthofen.

1918   Is home in Munich for Christmas.

1919   Exhibits in Frankfurt and Hanover (35 and 122 works respectively). Rents a studio in the Schlösschen Suresnes in Munich. Despite the efforts of Oskar Schlemmer and Willy Baumeister, fails to obtain a teaching position at the Stuttgart Academy of Fine Arts.

1920   Publishes his "Creative Credo" in the "Tribüne der Kunst und Zeit." His "Candide" is published by Kurt Wolff. Appointed professor at the Weimar Bauhaus.

1921   Settles in Weimar. Death of his mother, who has been paralyzed for twenty years, in Bern.

1922   Vacations on the island of Baltrum in the North Sea. Renews his contract with Goltz.

1923   Publication of his "Ways of Studying Nature" in a Bauhaus anthology. Exhibits in Berlin.

1924   First exhibition in the United States. Founds *Die Blauen Vier* with Feininger, Jawlensky, and Kandinsky. Trip to Sicily. Lectures on modern art in Jena. Has a visit from Léon-Paul Fargue. The Weimar Bauhaus is closed.

1925   The Bauhaus moves to Dessau, where Klee shares a house with Kandinsky. Publication of his "Pedagogical Sketchbook" in the "Bauhausbücher" series. Participates in the Surrealist exhibition at the Galerie Pierre in Paris. Has his first one-man exhibition in Paris, at the Galerie Vavin-Raspail.

1926   Trip to Italy (Island of Elba, Pisa, Ravenna, Florence).

1927   Trip to France (Porquerolles, Corsica, Avignon).

1928   Trip to Brittany and Belle-Ile-en-Mer. Publication of his "Exact Experiments in the Realm of Art" in "Bauhaus: Zeitschrift für Gestaltung". Third major trip that winter, to Egypt (Cairo, Luxor, Thebes, etc.).

1929   Continues travels in Egypt. One-man exhibition at Galerie Georges Bernheim in Paris. Visits the south of France, Gulf of Gascony, Bayonne, and Carcassonne. Major exhibition in Berlin.

1930   Another exhibition in Berlin; it travels to the Museum of Modern Art in New York. Klee spends some time in the

Engadine and at Viareggio in Italy. Exhibitions in Dresden, Düsseldorf, and Saarbrücken.

1931 Cancels his contract with the Bauhaus before its expiration. Teaches at the Academy of Fine Arts in Düsseldorf, where he exhibits 252 works. Vacations in Sicily; Palermo, Agrigentum, Syracuse, Monreale, and Ragusa.

1932 Spends some time in Switzerland and northern Italy (Venice).

1933 Klee loses his teaching post as a result of Nazi pressure. Visits the French Riviera (Port-Cros, Hyères, Saint-Raphaël, etc.). Leaves Germany for good and goes back to live in Bern.

1934 Kahnweiler succeeds Flechtheim as Klee's dealer.

1935 Retrospective in Bern. First attacks of scleroderma.

1936 Takes cures at Montana and Tarasp.

1937 Braque visits him in the spring. Klee spends the summer at Ascona. Has a visit from Picasso in the fall. One hundred and two of his works are confiscated in Germany; 17 are listed in the catalog of the "degenerate art" exhibit in Munich.

1938 Two one-man exhibitions in Paris, at the Louis Carré and Simon galleries. Spends the summer at Saint Beatenberg. Exhibition in New York.

1939 Spends some time at the Lake of Morat. In Geneva, visits the Prado exhibition (Goya, Velásquez, El Greco, etc.). Exhibition in Lucerne.

1940 Klee's father, Hans, dies on January 10. Major exhibition in Zurich, covering last five years of his work. On May 10 he is brought to the hospital in Locarno-Orselina. June 29, Paul Klee dies at the hospital of Locarno-Muralto in the Tessin. His remains are cremated on July 1, in Lugano. July 4, Klee memorial service in Bern. Several years later the urn containing his ashes is transferred to the cemetery of Schosshalden.

BIBLIOGRAPHY

MAIN WRITINGS BY PAUL KLEE

BOOKS

Pädagogisches Skizzenbuch. Munich: Albert Lagen, 1924.

Über die moderne Kunst. Bern: Benteli, 1945.

Dokumente und Bilder aus den Jahren 1896-1930. Berne: Benteli, 1949.

Graphik. Bern: Klipstein & Kornfeld, 1956.

Tagebücher von Paul Klee 1898-1918. Ed. by Felix Klee. Cologne: DuMont, 1957. *The Diaries of Paul Klee.* Berkeley and Los Angeles: University of California Press, 1964.

Gedichte. Ed. by Felix Klee. Zurich: Die Arche, 1960.

Some Poems by Paul Klee. Ed. by Anselm Hollo. Suffolk: Scorpio, 1962.

Das bildnerische Denken and *Unendliche Naturgeschichte.* Ed. by Jürg Spiller. Basel, Stuttgart: Schwabe, 1964, 1970. *The Notebooks of Paul Klee.* Vol. I, *The Thinking Eye.* Trans. by Ralph Mannheim. Vol. II, *The Nature of Nature.* Trans. by Heinz Norden. New York: Wittenborn, 1961, 1973.

Schriften, Rezensionen und Aufsätze. Ed. by Christian Geelhaar. Cologne: DuMont, 1976.

Briefe an die Familie 1893-1940. Ed. by Felix Klee. Cologne: DuMont, 1979.

Beiträge zur bildnerischen Formlehre. Anhang zum faksimilierten Originalmanuskript von Paul Klees erstem Vortragzyklus am Staatlichen Bauhaus Weimar 1921/1922. Transcription and introduction by Jürgen Glaesemer. Basel, Stuttgart: Schwabe, 1979.

ARTICLES

"Die Ausstellung des Modernen Bundes im Kunsthaus Zürich", *Die Alpen*, VI (August 1912), 6, pp. 696-704.

"Antwort auf eine Rundfrage an die Künstler: über den Wert der Kritik", *Der Ararat* , II (1921), p. 130.

"Wege des Naturstudiums", *Staatliches Bauhaus in Weimar 1919-1923*, Weimar, Munich: Bauhausverlag, 1923, pp. 24-25.

"Kandinsky", *Katalog der Jubiläumsausstellung zum 60. Geburtstag von W. Kandinsky*, Dresden: Galerie Arnold, 1926.

"Emil Nolde", *Festschrift für Emil Nolde anlässlich seines 60. Geburtstages*, Dresden: Neue Kunst Fides, 1927.

"Exakter Versuch im Bereich der Kunst", *Bauhaus, Zeitschrift für Gestaltung* II (1928), 2-3, p. 17.

"Huit poèmes", in Carola Giedion-Welcker, *Poèmes à l'écart. Anthologie der Abseitigen.* Bern: Benteli, 1946. Rev. ed., Zurich: Die Arche, 1964.

MONOGRAPHS

ABADIE, Daniel. *Paul Klee.* Paris: Maeght, 1978.

ALFIERI, Bruno. *Paul Klee.* Venice: Istituto Tipografico Editoriale, 1948.

ARMITAGE, Merle. *Five Essays on Paul Klee.* New York: Duell, Sloan & Pearce, 1950.

BAUMGARTNER, Marcel. *Paul Klee und die Photographie.* Bern: Kunstmuseum, 1979.

BENZ-ZAUNER, Margareta. *Werkanalytische Untersuchung zu den Tunisien Aquarellen Paul Klees,* Frankfurt, New York: P. Lang, 1984. Rev. ed. of the author's doctoral theses, Ludwig-Maximilians Universität, Munich, 1982.

BERNOULLI, Rudolf. *Mein Weg Zu Klee.* Bern: Benteli, 1940.

BLOESCH, Hans and SCHMIDT, Georg. *Paul Klee. Reden zu seinem Todestag 29 Juni 1940.* Bern: Benteli, 1940.

BRION, Marcel. *Paul Klee.* Paris: Somogy, 1955.

CASSOU, Jean. *Hommage à Paul Klee.* Boulogne-sur-Mer: L'Architecture d'aujourd'hui, 1949.

COOPER, Douglas. *Paul Klee.* Harmondsworth: Penguin Books, 1949.

COURTHION, Pierre. *Klee.* Paris: Hazan, 1953.

CREVEL, René. *Paul Klee.* Paris: Gallimard, 1930.

DORFLES, Gino. *Klee.* Milan: Del Millione, 1950.

DUVIGNAUD, Jean. *Klee en Tunisie.* Lausanne, Paris: Bibliothèque des arts, 1980.

FORGE, Andrew. *Paul Klee.* London: Faber & Faber, 1954.

GEELHAAR, Christian. *Paul Klee und das Bauhaus.* Cologne: DuMont, 1972. *Paul Klee and the Bauhaus.* Greenwich, Conn.: New York Graphic Society; Bath: Adams & Bart, 1973.

GEELHAAR, Christian. *Paul Klee. Leben und Werk.* Cologne: DuMont, 1974. *Paul Klee. Life and Work.* Trans. by W. Walter Jaffe. Woodbury, N.Y.: Barron's, 1982.

GEIST, Hans Friedrich. *Paul Klee.* Hamburg: Hauswedel, 1948.

GIEDION-WELCKER, Carola. *Paul Klee.* London: Faber & Faber; New York: Viking, 1952.

GIEDION-WELCKER, Carola. *Paul Klee in Selbstzeugnissen und Bilddokumenten.* Hamburg: Rowohlt, 1961.

GLAESEMER, Jürgen. *Paul Klee, Handzeichnungen.* 3 vol. Bern: Kunstmuseum, 1973-1984.

GLAESEMER, Jürgen. *Paul Klee: die farbigen Werke im Kunstmuseum Bern.* 2 vol. Bern: Kornfeld, 1976-1984.

GROHMANN, Will. *Paul Klee.* Paris: Cahiers d'Art, 1929.

GROHMANN, Will. *Paul Klee, Handzeichnungen, 1921-1930.* Potsdam, Berlin: Müller & Kiepenheuer, 1934.

GROHMANN, Will. *Paul Klee.* Stuttgart: Kohlhammer; New York: Abrams, 1954.

GROHMANN, Will. *Paul Klee, Handzeichnungen.* Cologne: DuMont, 1959. *Paul Klee. Drawings.* New York: Abrams, 1960.

GROHMANN, Will. *Der Maler Paul Klee.* Cologne: DuMont, 1966. New York, 1967.

GROHMANN, Will. *Paul Klee.* Paris: Nouvelles Editions françaises, 1977.

GROTE, Ludwig. *Erinnerungen an Paul Klee.* Munich: Prestel, 1959.

HAFTMANN, Werner. *Paul Klee. Wege bildnerischen Denken.* Munich: Prestel, 1950. *The Mind and Work of Paul Klee.* New York: Praeger, 1954. London: Faber & Faber, 1967.

HAUSENSTEIN, Wilhelm. *Kairuan oder eine Geschichte vom Maler Klee und von der Kunst dieses Zeitalters.* Munich: Wolff, 1921.

HAXTHAUSEN, Charles Werner. *Paul Klee. The Formative Years.* New York: Garland, 1981. Rev. ed. of the author's doctoral thesis, Columbia University, New York, 1976.

HENRY, Sara Lynn. *Nature and Modern Science, the 1920s.* Unpublished doctoral thesis, University of California, Berkeley, 1976.

HUGGLER, Max. *Paul Klee. Dokumente in Bildern II, 1930-1940.* Bern: Benteli, 1960.

HUGGLER, Max. *The Drawings of Paul Klee.* Alhambra: Borden, 1965.

HUGGLER, Max. *Paul Klee. Die Malerei als Blick in den Kosmos.* Frauenfeld: Huber, 1969.

HULTON, Nika. *An Approach to Paul Klee.* London: Phoenix, 1956.

JAFFE, Hans. *Klee.* London, New York: Hamlyn, 1971.

JORDAN, Jim M. *Paul Klee and Cubism 1912-1926.* Princeton: Princeton University Press, 1984. Rev. ed. of the author's doctoral thesis, New York University, 1974.

KAGAN, Andrew A. *Klee. Studies.* Unpublished doctoral thesis. Harvard University, 1977.

KAGAN, Andrew A. *Paul Klee. Art and Music.* Ithaca, New York; London: Cornell University Press, 1983.

KAHNWEILER, Daniel-Henry. *Klee.* Paris: Braun, 1950.

KLEE, Felix. *Paul Klee, Leben und Werk in Dokumenten.* Zurich: Diogenes, 1960. *Paul Klee: His Life and Work in Documents.* New York: Braziller, 1962.

KLEE, Felix. *Paul Klee.* Freiburg, Basel, Vienna: Rosenwind, 1984.

KORNFELD, Eberhard W. *Verzeichnis des graphischen Werkes von Paul Klee.* Bern: Kornfeld & Klipstein, 1963.

KORNFELD, Eberhard W. *Paul Klee in Bern.* Bern: Kornfeld & Klipstein, 1973.

KROLL, Christina. *Die Bildtitel Paul Klees.* Bonn: Rheinische Friedrich-Wilhelms-Universität, 1968.

KUENZI, André. *Paul Klee.* Martigny: Fondation Pierre Gianadda, 1980.

LANG, Lothar. *Paul Klee: Die Zwitschermaschine und andere Grotesken.* Berlin: Eulenspiegel, 1981.

LAXNER, Uta. *Stylanalytische Untersuchung zu den Aquarellen der Tunisreise 1914: Macke, Klee, Moilliet.* Bonn: Rheinische Friedrich-Wilhelms-Universität, 1967.

LYNTON, Norbert. *Klee.* London: Hamlyn, 1964.

MEHRING, Walter. *Klee.* Bern: Scherz, 1956.

MÜLLER, Joseph-Emile. *Klee: Carrés magiques.* Paris: Hazan, 1956.

NAUBERT-RISER, Constance. *La Création chez Paul Klee: étude de la relation théorie-praxis de 1900 à 1924. Paris, Ottawa: Klincksieck, 1978.

NIERENDORF, Karl. *Paul Klee, paintings, watercolors 1913-1939.* New York: Oxford University Press, 1941.

PETITPIERRE, Petra. *Aus der Malkasse von Paul Klee.* Bern: Benteli, 1957.

PLANT, Margaret. *Paul Klee: Figures and Faces.* London: Thames & Hudson, 1978.

PONENTE, Nello. *Klee. Etude biographique et critique.* Geneva: Skira, 1960.

READ, Herbert. *Klee 1879-1940.* London: Faber and Faber, 1948.

ROETHEL, Hans Konrad. *Paul Klee.* Wiesbaden: Vollmer, 1955.

ROETHEL, Hans Konrad. *Paul Klee in München.* Bern: Stämpfli, 1971.

ROY, Claude. *Klee aux sources de la peinture.* Paris: Le Club français du Livre, 1963.

SAN LAZZARO, Gualtieri di. *Paul Klee.* London: Thames and Hudson, 1967.

SCHMALENBACH, Werner. *Paul Klee: Fische.* Stuttgart: Reclam, 1958.

SCHMALENBACH, Werner. *Paul Klee: Die Düsseldorfer Sammlung.* Munich: Prestel, 1986.

SCHMIDT, Georg. *Paul Klee: Engel bringt das Gewünschte.* Baden-Baden: Woldemar Klein, 1957.

SHORT, Robert. *Paul Klee.* London: Thames & Hudson, 1979.

SOBY, James Thrall. *The Prints of Paul Klee.* New York: Curt Valentin, 1945.

THÜRLEMANN, Félix. *Paul Klee. Analyse sémiotique de 3 peintures.* Lausanne: L'Age d'Homme, 1982.

TOWER, Beeke Sell. *Klee and Kandinsky in Munich and at the Bauhaus.* Ann Arbor, Michigan: UMI Research Press, 1981.

VERDI, Richard. *Klee and Nature.* London: A. Zwemmer, 1984. New York: Rizzoli, 1985.

WEDDERKOP, Hermann von. *Paul Klee.* Leipzig: Klinkhardt & Biermann, 1920.

WERKMEISTER, Otto Karl. *Versuche über Paul Klee.* Francfort, 1981.

ZAHN, Leopold. *Paul Klee. Leben Werk, Geist.* Potsdam: Kiepenheuer, 1920.

ZAHN, Leopold. *Paul Klee in the Land Called Precious Stone.* Baden-Baden: Woldemar Klein, 1953.

1973 *Paul Klee. Paintings and Watercolors from the Bauhaus Years 1921-1931*. Des Moines Art Center. Int. by Marianne L. Teuber.

1974 1975 *Paul Klee. The Last Years, from the Collection of Felix Klee*. Museum and Art Gallery, Bristol; Hayward Gallery, London; Scottish National Gallery of Modern Art, Edinburgh.

1975 *Paul Klee. Das graphische und plastische Werk*. Wilhelm-Lehmbruck Museum, Duisburg.
Paul Klee 1879-1940. Die Ordnung der Dinge. Württembergischer Kunstverein, Stuttgart. Cat. by Tilman Osterwold.

1975-1976 *Paul Klee. Bilder, Aquarelle, Zeichnungen, Sammlung Felix Klee*. Kunstverein, Brunswick. Cat. by Heinz Holtmann.

1977 *Paul Klee*. Musée Maeght, St. Paul de Vence.
Paul Klee. The Late Years 1930-1940. Serge Sabarsky Gallery, New York.
Paul Klee at the Guggenheim Museum. The Solomon R. Guggenheim Museum, New York; Museum of Fine Arts, Montreal; Milwaukee Art Museum; Cleveland Museum of Art; Baltimore Museum of Art; Virginia Museum of Fine Arts, Richmond. Texts by Louise Averell Svendsen and Thomas M. Messer.
Paul Klee 1879-1940. Aquarelle, Zeichnungen, Graphik. Kunsthandlung Wittroch, Düsseldorf.
Paul Klee. Gemälde und Zeichnungen. Arnoldi-Livie, Munich.

1978-1980 *Paul Klee. Späte Arbeiten 1934-1940, aus der Sammlung Felix Klee*. Kunstmuseum, Bern; Kunsthalle, Bielefeld; Kestner Gesellschaft, Hannover. Text by Erich Franz.

1979 *A Tribute to Paul Klee*. National Gallery of Canada, Ottawa; Art Gallery of Ontario, Toronto. Text by David Burnett.
Paul Klee 1879-1940. Worthington Galleries, Chicago.
Honoring the Centenary of Paul Klee. Saidenberg Gallery, New York.
Paul Klee Centennial. Prints and Transfer Drawings. Museum of Modern Art, New York. Text by Howerdena Pindell.
Paul Klee. Fifty Prints. Stanford University Art Gallery, California. Cat. by Betsy G. Fryberger.
Paul Klee. Das Werk der Jahre 1919-1933. Gemälde, Handzeichnungen, Druckgraphik. Kunsthalle, Cologne. Cat. by Siegfried Gohr.
Paul Klee. Ausstellung schweizer Tage. Villa Schneider, Ingelheim am Rhein.
Klee und Kandinsky. Staatsgalerie, Stuttgart.

1979-1980 *Paul Klee. Das Frühwerk 1893-1922*. Städtische Galerie im Lenbachhaus, Munich. Cat. by Armin Zweite et al.
Paul Klee. Ein Kind träumt sich. Württembergischer Kunstverein, Stuttgart. Cat. by Tilman Osterwold.

1980 *Panorama de l'œuvre de Paul Klee*. Palais des Beaux-Arts, Charleroi.
Paul Klee. Gemälde, Aquarelle, Zeichnungen aus dem Besitz von Felix Klee. Hessisches Landesmuseum, Darmstadt.

Paul Klee. Sammlung Felix Klee. Kestner Gesellschaft, Hannover.
Paul Klee. Gemälde, farbige Blätter, Zeichnungen, Druckgraphische Werke. Die Sammlung Sprengel, die Sammlungen der Landeshauptstadt Hannover und des Landes Niedersachsen. Kunstmuseum, Hannover. Cat. by Bernd Bau.
Paul Klee. National Gallery of Ireland, Dublin.

1981 *Paul Klee. Opere 1900-1940, della collezione Felix Klee*. Orsanmichele, Florence.
Paul Klee. Oleos, acuarelas, dibujos y grabados. Fundación Juan March, Madrid.
Chefs-d'œuvre du Musée des Beaux-Arts de Berne: F. Hodler, P. Klee. Musée cantonal des Beaux-Arts, Lausanne.
Paul Klee. Museo de Arte Contemporaneo, Caracas.

1981-1982 *Paul Klee. Innere Wege*. Wilhelm Hack Museum, Ludwigshafen. Cat. by Manfred Fath and Elmar Bauer.

1982 *Paul Klee. L'Annunciazione del segno. Disegni e acquarelli*. Galerie Marescalchi, Milan. Text by Achille Bonito Oliva.

1983 *Paul Klee*. Jahrhunderthalle, Höchst, G.F.R.
Klee 1914-1940. Galerie Marisa del Re, New York. Text by Carmine Benincasa.
Paul Klee 1879-1940. His Life and Work. Art Gallery, Nottingham; Museum of Modern Art, Oxford.
The Graphic Legacy of Paul Klee. Bard College, Annandale on Hudson, New York.

1984 *Paul Klee. Œuvres de 1933 à 1940*. Musée des Beaux-Arts, Nîmes.

1984-1985 *Paul Klee*. Staatlichen Kunstsammlungen Kupferstich-kabinett, Dresden, G.D.R.

1985 *Paul Klee*. Fondation Pierre Gianadda, Martigny. Cat. by André Kuenzi.
Klee et la musique. Fondation Sonja Henie-Niels Onstad, Bærun, Norway; Musée National d'Art Moderne, Centre Georges Pompidou, Paris.
Paul Klee: les dix dernières années. Karl Flinker Gallery, Paris.

1985-1986 *Paul Klee in Exile 1933-1940*. Himeji City Museum of Art; Miyagi Museum of Arts; Museum of Modern Art, Kamakura; Museum of Modern Art, Shiga; Niigata City Art Museum.
Paul Klee als Zeichner 1921-1933. Bauhaus Archiv, Berlin; Städtsche Galerie im Lenbachhaus, Munich; Kunsthalle, Bremen. Cat. by Peter Hahn, Wolfgang Kersten Magdalena Drostel.

1986 *Paul Klee. Spätwerke 1937-1940*. Bünder Kunstmuseum, Chur. Cat. by Marcel Baumgartner by Beat Stutzer.
Paul Klee nelle collezioni private. Museo d'arte moderna Ca' Pesaro, Venice. Cat. by Sylvia Rathke-Köhl.

1987 *Paul Klee. Figurative Graphics from the Djerassi Collection*. San Francisco Museum of Modern Art.

1987-1988 *Paul Klee*. Museum of Modern Art, New York; Cleveland Museum of Art; Kunstmuseum, Bern. Cat. by Carolyn Lanchner.

ILLUSTRATIONS